WITHDRAWN

The States and the Metropolis

The States and the Metropolis

Lee S. Greene

Malcolm E. Jewell

Daniel R. Grant

University of Alabama Press

UNIVERSITY, ALABAMA

Contents

Preface

THIS VOLUME CONTAINS FIVE PAPERS DELIVERED
as the twenty-second annual lecture series for the Southern Regional Training Program in Public Administration.
In 1944, the Universities of Alabama, Georgia, and Tennessee, in co-operation with the Tennessee Valley Authority, inaugurated the Southern Regional Training Program.
In 1945, the University of Kentucky joined the program, replacing Georgia, and the Program has continued ever since under the auspices of the Universities of Alabama, Tennessee, and Kentucky. SRTP is unique in a great many ways. Not the least of its distinctions is the fact that it began with the support of a foundation grant but has survived the termination of that grant by many years.

A major feature of the Program is its lecture series, held in the fall of each year, which has brought to the University of Alabama campus outstanding students and practitioners of public administration for lectures before student–faculty groups and for conferences with the Fellows of the SRTP. Usually the speakers have reduced their lectures to written form, and the resulting books have been published by the University of Alabama Press.

The lectures comprising the present book were originally presented on the Alabama campus between October 31 and November 4, 1966. For the first time since 1944, the series was cast in the form of a symposium, with "The States and the Metropolis" as the subject. The first lecture was presented by Lee S. Greene, who is Distinguished Professor and Head, Department of Political Science, and Director, The Bureau of Public Administration, The University of Tennessee. The second and third lectures were delivered by Malcolm E. Jewell, Professor of Political Science, University of Kentucky. The final two lectures were presented by Daniel R. Grant, Professor of Political Science, Vanderbilt University, who also was an SRTP Fellow for 1945–46.

These authors require no further introduction; each is well known as a scholar and consultant. Nor do their topics require elaboration, for each presents a facet of the present status of the states and the American metropolis. The Bureau of Public Administration is pleased to have been the University agency through which this symposium was planned and brought to realization.

ROBERT B. HIGHSAW

University, Alabama
June 1, 1967

The States and the Metropolis

I

The Condition of the States

Lee S. Greene

MY ASSIGNMENT IN THIS SERIES OF LECTURES is to consider the general condition of the states. After I have accepted a task such as this, and the initial euphoria of cupidity and conceit has diminished, I think of Glendower and Hotspur. Says Glendower: "I can call spirits from the vasty deep," and Hotspur counters: "Why, so can I, or so can any man; but will they come when you do call for them?" One can call up ideas, but do they come when I do call them? As ideas developed, such as I *had* or could *find*, I inevitably found myself heavily concerned with the states' situation in the federal system. It is hard to say which is more pathetic—the academic apologist for the existing order (whatever is, is right) or the futile critic of everything (whatever is, is wrong). This being the case, I propose to adopt the role which is the more congenial to my temperament, that of unfriendly critic—a role I shall nevertheless attempt to keep within reasonable bounds. Unfortunately, the critic still needs, I think, an explanation, because the march of events has an air of inevitability that reminds me of the little boy's essay on Elisha:

Some boys made fun of Elisha's bald head. And he
said if you do that again I will have the bears eat you.
And they did. And he did. And the bears did.

It is, perhaps, the job of the critic who does not willingly
accept inevitability to propose a pause in the march of
events or a change of direction. He should not be sur-
prised if he is ineffective. But his criticisms need not
cease, for his principal task is not to reform or to alter, but
to comment. This is a modest role but a useful one, most
appropriate to a professed educator.

Clearly one cannot speak on the American states today
without saying something on the subject of federal–state
relations, and as impossible as it is to avoid this subject, it
is almost equally impossible to say anything new unless
one adopts the stance of a complete crackpot—and even
this is not *very* new. I have accepted a frustrating assignment, for the condition of the states is such that one
hardly knows what to say. What good are the states any-
way? One of the hackneyed words of my profession these
days (we have a great many) is "viable." On the basis of
many usages of this word, doubts may be raised whether
our states are viable, but I do not intend to devote much
space to this question. The states of the United States are
historical happenings. At first, the political structures on
the East Coast must have seemed fairly logical and reasonable. The pattern that was started there began to be
repeated, and the process was kept up. Boundaries often
seemed to have little reference to anything except surveyors' conveniences. But, if the process of state creation
offered little resemblance to any careful program of what,
in present-day "grantese," would undoubtedly be called
"felt needs," at least it can be said that it was no worse

than the creation of states in other parts of the world, where comparable political structures have been created by marriage, conquest, accidents, misguided nationalism, and all the other human circumstances that give rise to decisions. Viable or not, in any ideal sense, the states seem certain to remain. Indeed, it is exceedingly difficult to get rid of *any* governmental unit in the United States. I noted a year or so ago the published annual report of a Kansas township near my former home. The township had a government. It had fluid assets of $92.00. During the year it had spent $16.42, of which amount the publication of the annual report had used $12.42, leaving a sum of $4.00 to be spent for the rental of the Coonhunters Hall. One can hardly describe this township as viable, yet it was alive—barely—and apparently had a modest recreation program.

The Growth of Federal Activity

It is not, however, very satisfying to settle for the idea that states will continue to exist merely because it is impossible to get rid of them, although I think one might also say this about many nation–states. One would like to feel, I suppose, that a better justification could be found for the states, and some political scientists, at least, feel an uncontrollable itch to search for moralistic reasons for things as they are or as they *should* and *could* be. A good bit of print, over a longer period of time than one might think today, has been devoted to the question of the future of the states and their reason for being. Elsewhere in this volume Dr. Grant retraces for us the ways foreseen by gloomy prophets. Presumably the continued existence of the states may be justified partly on the ground that the federal government cannot do everything. Unfortunately for any conviction that such a sentiment might carry, a good deal of activity occurs as though there were nothing at all in this idea. Whenever anything appears to need doing, demands are promptly made for federal action. Such demands come from all kinds of pressure groups, but, significantly, they also come from the states themselves and, more especially, from the localities. In late summer of 1966, as Senator Abraham Ribicoff and his colleagues started to probe the depths of federal influence on localities, Mayor John Lindsay was complaining that New York City had to have more federal money (although he was in no position to say clearly how much it was getting already), and Mayor Samuel Yorty was excusing the inactivity of Los Angeles on the ground of his lack of power, even while sharply calling Senator Robert Kennedy's attention to his ability to run "his" city without the Senator's advice.[1] It must be abundantly clear that the decentralized institutions expect to march on Washington in the posture of prayer as practiced by the classic Greeks—with palms outstretched—except when they are too sharply outraged by the social views of the central bureaucracy.

To me, it is distressing that the states and localities actively seek federal aid even in some areas where such aid need not be asked. I know that by voicing such a sentiment I will invite the disapprobation of some of my colleagues, especially at a time when staff, buildings, equipment, and even furniture for academicians are being purchased with national funds. Nevertheless, I think it true that the states and localities can avoid passing all their responsibilities away. A recent proposal has appeared especially unnecessary to me, as an example of the kind of thing I have in mind; I refer to the training of state and local government officials. The training function is one that is peculiarly close to an agency. Leaving aside, for the moment, the question of pre-service training, it seems clear that the continued training of personnel is the responsibility of the agency whose staff is involved. From this point of view the state and the local units, perhaps acting in concert, have full responsibility for providing their own training. I find it quite impossible to believe that the states cannot themselves afford to supply this training. For many years they have provided extensive educational systems for the general public; surely they can find the funds for the much narrower programs of public service training. Nevertheless, representatives of the states and the localities have persistently urged the necessity for federal money for this purpose and have succeeded in getting some, although they are by no means satisfied with what they have received so far. In so doing they have once again placed themselves in the position of having to guess whether the particular programs they propose will be acceptable to some federal granting agency. The prospects of consistent, long-range training programs in such a situation are bound to be clouded.

Let me turn slightly aside to pay my disrespects to certain aspects of federal–university relationships as they are developing. This area merits the attention of congressional investigation; I would like to suggest some lines of inquiry. The universities have begun to appeal to the national politician as mechanisms for getting something —even anything—done. Unmindful of or inattentive to the fact that the university with only a limited budget already has its hands full trying to oblige ever larger numbers of students, the federal agency typically looks to the university to start something new, imaginative, and precedent-breaking. Furthermore, the typical federal agency has all the faults of a foundation, plus some special ones of its own. It adopts no specific program; it enters instead a fuzzy area of difficulty often as wide as the great globe itself and invites the universities to plan and submit research or action projects. Senator Ribicoff feels that federal urban policy lacks coordination; would that he might take a look at federal–university research. Federal agencies have no considered stable social policy in making grants. Their policies, such as they are, waver and change as they have in the programs established under the National Defense Education Act; little consistency or certainty is maintained. Universities already well blessed with money and staff often get more money, and hence more and better staff. For example, the Agency for International Development and its predecessors have been captivated and partially captured by certain institutions, which have vigorously milked the contract cow. We are in for more of this, perhaps, if present federal legislation to aid universities in world-affairs studies is funded.

So much for the notion that the federal government cannot do everything. If this idea once prevailed, it has gone at least partially into eclipse of late. We are now more fully committed to the notion that the federal government can do everything—all at once.[2]

The Justification of States

In my youth, the states were often justified on the grounds that they furnished "laboratories" for experimentation. One hears somewhat less of this notion nowadays, but as recently as 1961 Morton Grodzins referred to the idea in a Rand McNally essay series, although his examples were rather more historic than current.[3] Wisconsin and Minnesota once experimented with such things as civil service, commission regulation of utilities, and the income tax. New York experimented with public control or provision of housing. Kansas experimented with the control of labor unions. A number of states experimented with prohibition of liquor and tobacco. And, of course, there were some experiments with more disastrous results. Part of the country experimented with human slavery;[4] and most of it experimented with child labor and low wages. But if we are to make a virtue of variety, we must reconcile ourselves to evil as well as good. In Grodzins' terms, the "successful" experiments of the states were followed by national action, and hence the states appear as innovators.

I think it would be an exaggeration to leave the impression that states and localities have entirely ceased experimenting or that they are totally lacking in initiative. In the troubled field of racial adjustment, some states and localities have, somewhat on their own, taken steps to ameliorate poor conditions. Years before the current wave of federal legislation and federal administrative action, my own southern city had integrated the bus lines and the airport restaurant. After the federal government had begun to move, but before compulsion was the rule, Knoxville developed an open–city policy for restaurants and hotels with some considerable success and succeeded in avoiding excessive demonstration trouble. Of course, racial problems in Knoxville do not affect as many people as they do in some areas, but, all the same, the city and its administration are entitled to some credit. New York State is experimenting with types of pollution control. A number of states had attempted "fair employment" or other non-discrimination legislation well before Congress nationalized the program. Perhaps, indeed, experimentation is as vigorous at the state and local level as it ever was. I find it difficult to tell whether this is so or not.

It may be that "experimentation" by the states, even when it exists, makes little impression because it is often lacking in forcefulness. Let me give a few examples. In Tennessee we are already cluttering our beautiful new interstate highways with billboards—bigger, better, and higher. In urban areas especially, the high-rise billboards are up before the throughways are opened to traffic. On a snowy night, when the gas needle flutters on the extreme left, the sight of a high-rise Texaco or Esso sign may be more satisfying than Mt. LeConte in the autumn haze, but such occasions are rare. Most of the time, such constant insistence on consumers' needs are around too much. (On the other hand, some localities are, on their own initiative, awakening to the importance of aesthetic values, as in Charleston, South Carolina, or Savannah, Georgia, where extensive restorations of unique examples of architecture and city planning are now in progress.)

Or take pollution. What have the cities ever done in these matters? I recall that some years ago the secretary of our municipal association was proposing—seriously, I presume—that TVA pay for sewerage control, on the ground that TVA's interference with the river's flow had upset the hitherto spasmodic aeration provided for municipal raw sewage. Or what have the states done to control the waste-disposal programs of their own subdivisions? In this field we have had to wait for federal threats. Dr. Grant's essay notes the increasing truculence and determination of the federal government, clearly foreshadowed by the following statement of an assistant secretary of the United States Department of Health, Education, and Welfare:

> But let me make something clear. While I use the word "invitation" deliberately, you should be warned that I define it rather broadly. We might, for example, consider ourselves invited to start an enforcement action in your area without ever receiving a communication on the engraved stationery of the Governor of your State. We might on occasion consider ourselves invited if we heard nothing from your State, especially when that lack of communication was matched by an equal lack of State action to meet a long-standing pollution problem of major proportion.
>
> So that there can be no misunderstanding, let me state it clearly. The best way to keep us out of your State is to get that pollution out of your water. If you can't and want us to help, we will be happy to try. If you don't, we may be forced to try even though you don't want us to.
>
> You might not believe it, but it is a fact that I happen to be a firm believer in States' rights. I also happen to believe with equal firmness, however, in States' responsibilities, and to put it frankly too many States have not faced up to their responsibilities in the matter of water pollution control. This is understandable. Water pollution problems are often problems that are not easy to solve, and when solutions are found they are often expensive to implement.[5]

The quietude of the states is often justified on the grounds that they cannot act, either because of fear of loss in the competitive race with other states, or simply because they don't have the resources. But acceptance of the first justification—that Tennessee, for example, cannot control the weight of trucks on its highways because Alabama won't—disposes completely of the notion of experimentation. Experimentation involves risk-taking. The other excuse—that financial resources are not available—is highly suspect. Surely, when a major economic storm hits the country or the world, the state's fiscal powers avail little. But, as Dr. Grant points out, the expenditures of the states are very substantial, and there are certainly many things which the states can do—on their own. By and large, I think the states can afford to limit water and air pollution; they can regulate billboards and preserve scenic resources; they can construct, operate, and finance decent parks; they can build university plants and pay teachers; they could, perhaps, redevelop cities and control slums, at least to some degree. For all of these programs they now accept federal money in a manner that seems to me increasingly greedy.

If the states cannot do these things, the cause for that inability is not entirely financial, I believe, but political. They cannot because, in a sense, they will not.

The Fate of Reform

Proposals to return functions to the states or the localities have been made repeatedly in the last fifteen years, as Professor Grant has fully indicated in the pages which follow. The Eisenhower Administration, particularly, was accompanied by noises of this sort, and such proposals received honored attention in the spasms of self–study which distinguished the executive branch in that period, but nothing ever happened as the result of that organized introspection. Academic critics of my type have delivered manifestoes on this same matter from time to time, but an air of frustration and futility has surrounded the whole matter. Not only have functions not been returned to the states, but the tempo of federal intrusion has been so stepped up that it is no longer certain that *any* area of activity can be left primarily to state initiative, in spite of increased state expenditure. Perhaps the initiative of the future will consist in thinking of new ways to tap the national treasury.

The difficulty of finding functions suitable for state and local attention these days is well pointed up by noting that nothing of any significance escapes the attention of the national government. It seems impossible to find any exception. For example, one might initially suppose that air pollution in some localities would be a local problem, but it is at once apparent that in many important areas it has interstate (not to say international) implications. Even more so, one might have said that local government is a state concern, and so it is, in a strictly legal way. But, viewed realistically, local conditions are now of great interest to the national government. Two significant directions of pressure have helped to bring this about. The urban areas have clearly become dissatisfied with the support, financial and otherwise, that they can secure from their states, and they have conducted much the same kind of "march on Washington" that every other pressure group attempts. Secondly, it has become increasingly clear in Washington that the federal government must act through the local units and must therefore be concerned with what these units are and how they behave. The preliminary surveys of Senator Ribicoff in the fall of 1966 indicate with some force the confusion in Washington as well as in the field. And the mayors, having pressed Washington for money, are now discovering the pleasures of senatorial instruction offered from a bench bathed in immunity. Washington has helped to create—and continues to exacerbate—the problems of metropolitan coordination. It should be entertaining, even if not instructive, to watch it struggle with the search for solutions.

Negation as a Role

Circumstances have provided a curious role for the states. At first glance it seems a poor one, but I believe we need to examine it with more care. This role is the negative one of protest against change and innovation. Both Grodzins and Daniel Elazar have emphasized the partnership of the states and the national government in making policy and carrying out programs. And Elazar, like Grodzins, mentions a few instances in which states have shown some initiative in undertaking actions which the national government had evaded. But, as Elazar himself reluctantly admits, "Unfortunately, the more spectacular examples of the power of the states within the cooperative framework tend to reflect obstructionism (or something akin to it)." [6] He cites a number of small schemes for state or local frustration of federal policy. On initial examination this frustrating role of the states appears unfortunate, at least to persons who believe that change is both right and necessary. The spectacle of gubernatorial campaigns fought and won on platforms of mere resistance to federal programs is distressing and disquieting. It is hard to arouse enthusiasm in a country so devoted as ours is to ideas of progress and dynamic action for a political platform consisting entirely of the word "No," spelled out in a variety of ways. But, it seems increasingly clear that there *is* a negative side. It is only a bit unfortunate that the states have become primarily the agencies to take the part of delay and denial. Whether or not the states are right in assuming a negative role in any particular issue depends entirely on one's own values; but it is well to remember (what political scientists frequently forget, I fear) that often a case can be made for inaction.

Perhaps the greatest value of the states lies in their support of pluralism, for there can be little doubt that a powerful national government is bound to seek some uniformity and, to that degree, a kind of totalitarianism.[7] And to the extent that the national government can follow an internally consistent policy, the danger of totalitarianism is increased. The dangers of federal domination have been so often reiterated that political scientists would be reluctant to discuss the matter, except that in the nature of things political scientists must accustom themselves to hackneyed subjects. (After all, political science goes back at least to Socrates.) A further excuse for talking about this matter lies in the need for repetition as a public service. Now a subject may become embarrassing because it has been adopted for the wrong reasons or because it has been promoted by unpleasant people, and the question of Federal domination is embarrassing on both counts. I probably do not need to expand on this point. Almost anyone can pick up a handy and distasteful opponent who has talked about federal domination, because such domination has been the object of fear and distrust since the Articles of Confederation. It is possible, however, that the matter has lately acquired some new aspects, perhaps in part because it now involves the wide-

spread notion that government ought to cure evil in all its
forms. If pushed to its ultimate, by applying what a friend
of mine calls "the law of imaginary horribles," this could
lead to a kind of creeping totalitarianism.*

A case in point is a recent flurry over the treatment of
the Negro in textbooks. Newspaper columnists of the
alarmist persuasion are beginning to suggest that federal
bureaucrats will use the money power to compel the
adoption of texts approved as to the adequacy of their
treatment of the Negro. Is this possible? I don't really
know, but we are living through a time when employment
practices of private persons are, and perhaps the sale of
property by private persons will be, supervised by governmental means in the name of racial nondiscrimination,
and the step from this standard to that of textbook selec-
tion may not be as great as one might think. In this
respect, at least, state independence and pluralism may
be better, simply on the theory that in a pluralistic situation, the truth and the moral may have an opportunity to
fight for survival, or even on the theory that the immoral
may continue its struggle.

I would like to quote some recent writing relevant to
this matter. Irving Kristol has said in *The National Observer* for October 24, 1966:

> First, on all the evidence, the one worst way to cope
> with this crisis in values is through organized politi-
> cal–ideological action. Most of the hysteria, much of
> the stupidity, and a good part of the bestiality of the
> Twentieth Century have arisen from efforts to do

* The literature of our day is filled with the imagined but grisly
conditions of computerized Utopias. Perhaps this is more than mere
literary sensationalism or neuroticism.

precisely this. Not only do such efforts fail; they fail
in the costliest fashion. And if modern history can be
said to teach anything, it is that, intolerable as the
crisis in values may be, it invariably turns out to be far
less intolerable than any kind of "final solution" imposed by direct political action.

But he then goes on to say:

Democracy, after all, means self-government; and
such self-government is, in the long run, utterly impossible without adequate self-definition, self-
certainty, self-control. All of modern life and modern
culture have combined to make the self a question to
itself. I regard it as utopian to expect that people will
not turn to politics for answers. And I regard it as
certain that they will take vicious answers rather than
none at all.

It may be that the attempted use of national powers to
hasten changes that are not fully acceptable to those who
can use the states as delaying devices will bring a renewed constitutional crisis in federal–state relations. It is
unfortunate that such a crisis should have cast the states
in a role that seems disagreeable in many ways, but it is
significant that, if such a crisis is now in the making, it
appears less and less likely, this time, to be an exclusively
North–South crisis.

A Lack of Issues

The relatively low interest in the states is reflected in
their politics. It would be an exaggeration to maintain
that no political issues trouble the calm stagnation of state
public life. Such issues do arise. I need not belabor the

major issue of Alabama policy—an issue which I think one may honestly say no longer so seriously troubles Alabama's neighbor to the north. This same issue is now all too clear in northern and western states, notably in the case of open housing. But while this is a political issue, it is not a partisan issue.

It is possible that state politics have never displayed striking issues. Questions on prohibition, women's suffrage, the voting age, and other such matters arise from time to time (in fact, liquor control is a hardy perennial), but strictly state issues haven't made much history. Even the vital state issues just suggested have been largely parts of national concerns. California has some issues at the moment, but they are principally national issues; even the budgetary crisis there has national overtones.

One might add, of course, that there may be more state issues than the general observer can be aware of, because they may exist locally without attracting any particular national attention. One must remember that issues are not necessarily required for partisan politics. A good portion of political struggle merely boils down to the question of the "ins" versus the "outs." The issues get settled by negotiations other than the electoral process. At the same time, the want of dramatic questions at the state level tends to raise doubts concerning the importance of state activity. Why not simply leave the whole business to the technician and the bureaucrat?

The mere improvement of the technical aspects of administration is not exactly a satisfactory substitute for political independence, except perhaps to the expert. A recent study of local affairs, made at the University of Tennessee, indicates that the liveliest political exchanges take place in those counties that maintain the lowest level of services.[8] This is significant in several ways, one of them being the fact that the low level of services is maintained deliberately. Were the states to become merely effective administrative machines, without political vitality, they could scarcely remain very lively political units. Already some of this sort of development has occurred.

I believe one should observe, too, that big and decisive issues do not necessarily indicate a healthy state of affairs. The political scientist naturally likes issues, because they increase his scope of investigation. The musician must have disharmony as a contrast to harmony. But the bigger the issues are, the greater the danger that the state cannot settle them at all. Portions of Africa are at the moment very well supplied with issues; perhaps we should not waste too much time lamenting the lack of political issues at the state level.

Are State–Local Functions Still Possible?

Have we reached the stage where no function, and no issue, can be considered as belonging clearly to the state? Chancellor Heard in a passage published for the American Assembly has said:

> The role of the states in education, if nothing else, makes the state legislature a crucial organ of government in our future. The character of the primary and secondary school systems of the country, and increasingly of the college and university systems, is determined importantly by the policies and appropriations of state legislatures. Federal funds for education, especially higher education, increased after 1957 and surged upward particularly in 1965. These funds, however, were usually specialized in character, de-

signed to aid specified groups or to encourage activities, like medical research, deemed by Congress important to the national interest. Deeper involvement by federal agencies in education notwithstanding, state legislatures seem destined to continue to control the bulk of public money going into educational instruction at all levels. As the interconnection of education with all aspects of a state's life continues to increase, the significance of legislative actions and attitudes in educational matters will also continue to rise. In all sorts of allied spheres, the arts for example, state legislative attitudes will also be important.[9]

But this judgment may be placed somewhat in doubt by current developments, not only because special programs backed by federal funds may upset state patterns, but also because the very fact of *co-ordination* of federal pressure may dominate state and local policy-making.

It is interesting, perhaps, to look at the policing function in the United States. On the European continent the control of the police has been centralized for a long time, under a system that emphasizes the importance of control of the central apparatus. Control of the police in Europe can be almost as important as control of the army; it was no accident that the growing Nazi party of the early 1930's headed straight for the control of the police. The Anglo–American tradition has been different. Policing—and the standards of law enforcement—have been highly localized. The same thing has characterized the practice of criminal law. In an Appalachian county in my state, just a few years ago, it was found impossible to secure a jury to sit on a trial for murder. Nothing could be done. Removal of the trial to some other place was impossible, unless the defendant wished it—and he didn't. The resulting collapse of proceedings was most distressing to many people, but some lawyers noted that we were presented with a rather unusual example of local determination of law enforcement.

So far we have maintained the attitude that law enforcement is highly local. Even the creation of *state* policing agencies has met with opposition and the activities of the state forces are often circumscribed. Do we now face the prospect of change in this area also? The civilian review board contest in New York City, which did furnish a local issue, attained wider significance. In the last presidential campaign, the dangers and disorders of the cities were made something of a campaign issue, although defenders of the former administration were quick to point out that the federal government had little responsibility. This, too, is changing, for now the Johnson Administration, again borrowing a plank from Senator Goldwater's campaign, is prepared to attack the problem of law enforcement by means of extensive federal grants to local police.[10]

Lost Opportunities

The history of federal–state relations is cluttered with cases of opportunities lost by the states. One such lost opportunity was the matter of legislative reapportionment, which Professor Jewell deals with in detail in later pages. Whatever need there may be for the protection of minorities, a completely rotten borough system such as Tennessee had (and I assume Tennessee was fairly typical) can have no justification in modern society. In Tennessee, no responsible authority with power, save one, did anything to reform the existing structure. The legislature itself did nothing, although its obligation was clear. Prior to *Baker* v. *Carr,* I heard a number of legislators speak slightingly and with laughter on the subject (a badly timed joke, as it turned out). The governors studiously avoided commitment, which, on the basis of the theory of separation of powers, they were certainly entitled to do, except for the fact that the theory of separation of powers has never much inhibited the Tennessee executive. The only exception to the general official inactivity was a Davidson County chancellor who anticipated, in his decision, the general attitude of *Baker* v. *Carr* and the subsequent decisions of the lower federal courts. The Tennessee Supreme Court itself scurried behind the hitherto firm wall of the "political question," and thus invited the intervention of a higher, more courageous, and more far-sighted judiciary. And the upshot of the whole business was a further expansion of federal judicial power.

Now, of course, to keep the record straight, it is necessary to note how difficult it is for institutions to reform themselves, as anyone familiar with university administration can readily observe. Local governmental units have been conspicuously unsuccessful in such matters. But such reform is not impossible. Even great reformations are possible. Japan abolished its feudal system by a powerful, significant, and swift act of will. Following the Protestant Reformation, the Roman Catholic Church undertook significant change, and it has been doing so again in our time. Self-reform may be rare, but it is not impossible, and in the matter of reapportionment the states have richly deserved the low prestige in which they are sometimes held.

Perhaps the states face one of their most crucial challenges in the field of urban government, since the urban units are officially the creatures of the state and are wholly subject to the state. It is widely supposed that the cities have been abused and neglected by the states—that they have repeatedly been left floundering by the states or have been restricted by them so that they could do nothing. Such an assumption may be partially true, but it is incomplete, for the relationship between the city and the state is far more complex than the simple mechanism suggested by the words "state" and "city." In Tennessee (and again I assume that the situation is not untypical) cities, that is, the city governments, would like to use the machinery of the state for their own advantage—to give themselves powers and, most of all, money—but they steadfastly resist the supervisory power of the state. It seems to me that, in return for money, the supervisory power of the federal government is more willingly accepted, perhaps because, except in the case of very powerful cities like Chicago or New York, the attempt to get the money without the supervision seems so hopeless.

Political Scientists and State–Local Studies

In spite of, or possibly because of, the position, perhaps unfortunate, in which the states find themselves, political scientists have increasingly concerned themselves with state and local affairs. This may not change much of anything, but then one can never tell for sure. In the resurgence of professional interest (not, to be sure, confined to political scientists) in state affairs, the American legislature has occupied a prominent place. (Dr. Jewell discusses this area in detail elsewhere in this volume.)

The state legislature has been distrusted for a long

time—at least since the 1850's. In 1949, the *Knoxville Journal* put the matter very clearly, and there is no reason to suppose that this point of view has changed:

> For our part, and we think many citizens will share our view, the sooner the Legislature closes the safer the state's population will feel. While every legislative body does some good and necessary things, the public welfare usually takes a good many beatings before any session is concluded.

Reformers, or would-be reformers, of the legislature, are likely to suggest, among other matters, the desirability of more frequent and longer sessions, as a means of enabling the legislature to assert a power more nearly equal to that of a professional and full-time governor. Such proposals occasion anxiety in some quarters. State legislatures have had their share of corruption and manipulation, but I believe it is the uncertainty of legislative output that troubles the constituency. And it must be admitted that this is a feature of the times—of the constant decision–making which robs us all of a sense of stability and permanence. It is not only the courts that can be accused of providing a one–way ticket for this place and date only.

The proposals for the improvement of the legislature generally are not very stirring, for they deal mostly with mechanics—procedure, the size of committees, office space, salaries, terms, and the like. I do not wish to be overly critical of such ideas—I have nothing any better to offer—and it is possible that improvements of this sort may elevate legislative prestige a bit. I remember in the 1953 Tennessee Constitutional Convention watching a committee of that constituent body—supposedly ranking third in the political hierarchy after God and the people—meekly vacating the Senate chamber in order to make way for a conference scheduled by the Comptroller in that room, and wandering in a bemused fashion around the hallway seeking some vacant corner where it might deliberate. I thought it an altogether sad spectacle. But mechanical improvements will not take the place of power, and it is the legislature's power and capacity that have suffered some eclipse.

Now, as a writer who has from time to time harped on the powers of the state executive (especially in Tennessee, where we have indeed had powerful and able governors for at least thirty years), I want to say that, upon reflection, I think I may have overdone it a bit. The state governor is often very powerful, and legislatures seem acquiescent, but the governor's power may rest upon a few powerful legislative leaders. In any case, in my own state the prospect of a highly independent legislature creates something of a general scare.

Thirty years ago we lived through a time of extensive interest in administration as the New Deal and World War II put unusual strains upon our capacity. Then, as now, the states and their interests were overshadowed by national concerns. The interest in administrative matters has, as we can all see, declined somewhat in the political science profession, and the word "politics" has taken on a renewed vitality. In the name of this new interest, discoveries are being announced, sometimes in territory that has long been fully occupied. The study of administration, as well as its practice, has been subject to some doubts and attacks. Nevertheless, it is admitted by all that the bureaucracy is, if anything, even more powerful than before and that it is not likely to become less so. The problems of administration have not gone away simply because our brethren have turned most of their attention to other matters. There are still things to be done.

An assumption can be easily made that the administrative performance at the federal level is superior to that of the states. This assumption is one that I have observed from time to time in the conversation of federal officials, and I assume that some state officials are willing, secretly, to accept it. The assumption ought to be examined. In truth, the federal administrative record is not always good. The size of the federal establishment has frequently defeated all attempts at co-ordination. The power of the federal bureaucracy has often enough prevented change and reform. Some of the advantages of federal service— the higher pay and the better retirement—can be attributed to a taxing power so formidable that it is well-nigh irresponsible.

The states and the localities have of course gone only part way in the direction of reform. Our administrative structure is in many cases still nonrationalized. Our merit-system coverage is still incomplete, and our personnel practices are imperfect. The fact that these subjects appear hackneyed does not preclude them from being important. The principal caution one might express on such matters could be said of the legislature as well: a government cannot be made vital merely by building up a smooth and admirable piece of machinery. A piece of machinery is made to do something or go somewhere.

I do not wish to carry the guilt of pride too far, and hence I do not want to overestimate the influence of college professors, but at the same time I do not care to downgrade it completely, and as we seek to bend the power of intellect to an examination of political affairs, not without some hope that we can influence events, so I would attribute some of the obscurity of state and local affairs to the failure of college teachers to attend to them. The national government has been, and is being, studied backwards and forwards, sideways and in depth, in warm weather and cold, macro and micro, with the full support of required courses and a market that shimmers like a rainbow in the dreams of publishers. The states and the localities have not fared so well. Lately our brother scholars have, indeed, begun to correct the imbalance, for clearly there is a resurgence of state and local political and functional studies. Nevertheless, the place of state and local political and administrative studies is a secondary one, and the neglect and disrespect accorded this area by the curriculum makers continues the ignorance and indifference of the citizen toward his own most immediate governments. They remain to him mysterious and unknown. For this neglect of a complex and difficult area the academic world must take some blame.

II

The Changing Political
Environment of
State Government

Malcolm E. Jewell

THIS IS A TIME OF POLITICAL CHANGE IN THE
American states. During the last few decades, massive
economic and social changes associated with metropolitan
and industrial growth have occurred, but until recently
they have not given rise to comparable changes in the
political life of the states. The structure of state and local
government and the character of state political forces
have remained relatively stable and almost immune to
those influences that have transformed the face of America since the 1920s. But today we are at last witnessing
political changes that are all the more rapid and chaotic
because they have been so long delayed. Within a period
of four years many of our largest cities have increased
their legislative representation by as much as five or ten
times, and hundreds of rural counties have lost their individual seats in the lower house. In the North, the Democratic Party has won unaccustomed majorities in a number of legislative bodies; in at least half a dozen southern
states, the Republican Party has made its first serious bid
for the governorship. Negro candidates have won local

elections in Alabama and legislative races in Georgia, but segregationist candidates have still profited from southern political trends. The problems of the metropolis, so long ignored, now dominate the newspaper headlines and the political campaigns: unemployment, delinquency, impoverished schools, and racial ghettos. Intermittent race riots in the nation's largest cities have exposed both the urgency and the explosive character of urban problems.

It is easy to provide examples of political ferment in the states; it is much more difficult to demonstrate that there is any pattern to this ferment or to predict the changes we may expect in state government and politics. The diversity of the American states frustrates our efforts to generalize about political change. States differ in traditions and political culture, in the pace of metropolitan growth, and in the relative strength of the political forces that are contesting for power. In every state there are changes in legislative apportionment and in party competition, but the effects of these changes will not be identical in any two states. We are searching for the most important and most extensive patterns of change, but we should have no illusions that our conclusions are equally accurate or pertinent to every state.

The Political Consequences of Legislative Reapportionment

By the summer of 1966, four years after the United States Supreme Court challenged malapportionment, and two years after it required that both legislative houses be apportioned on the basis of population equality, every state had reapportioned its legislature or was under judicial order to do so. The Court's decision has been implemented with more speed than deliberation. The congressional effort to limit the scope of judicially determined standards to a single branch of the legislature has been defeated. While judicially enforced reapportionment was still being debated in the law journals, the newspapers, and the legislative halls, it had become an accomplished fact. In the new legislatures this standard of population equality has been achieved or approximated.

The mathematical effects of reapportionment can be estimated easily, even though it is too early to calculate them with any precision. In 1961 a third or less of the electorate could, theoretically, choose a majority of over half of the upper houses and two-fifths of the lower branches; in most of the reapportionment plans that have gained judicial approval the minimum proportion is over 45 percent. In 1961 the value of the vote for legislatures across the country averaged more than twice as much in counties of under 25,000 population as it did in counties of over 500,000; in nine states the contrast was more than five to one.[1] Today reapportionment is roughly equalizing the value of the vote in large and small counties. The counties that have been the most underrepresented, and that are gaining most substantially, are the predominantly suburban ones. The cities and counties in the core of metropolitan areas have gained representation, often large numbers of seats, but few of them are increasing enough in population to gain seats in the years ahead. Relatively few states have increased the size of legislative bodies, and consequently urban and suburban gains have been made at the expense of rural counties. Large numbers of rural counties have been forced to combine with one or several others in the formation of House districts, and in many states large clusters of rural counties have been required for Senate districts. In short, reapportionment in many states has resulted in a rapid and massive transfer of legislative power from rural to metropolitan counties.

If we try to do more than measure the effects of reapportionment mathematically, we must explore the ways in which various patterns of apportionment affect partisan politics and the relationships between reapportionment and the other important political trends apparent in the states. Malapportionment is not likely to affect the balance of partisan power in the legislature unless one party draws its electoral support principally from metropolitan counties and the other party dominates the more rural counties. In the postwar period this situation has been characteristic of most of the northeastern and midwestern states. State Democratic parties, capitalizing on the urban appeal of the Roosevelt administration and traditional ethnic loyalties, have concentrated their voting strength in the metropolitan areas; the most consistent sources of Republican votes have been the rural counties, the towns, and the smaller cities. The operation of the district system of legislative elections has contributed to further bipolarization of the legislative parties; in most of these states, the Democratic Party has been overwhelmingly metropolitan and the Republican Party predominantly rural. Malapportionment has not had a comparable effect on partisan strength in the two-party states farther west because the constituency bases of the parties do not differ so substantially.

One effect of malapportionment, particularly in the northeastern and midwestern industrial states, has been to increase the likelihood of divided government. Democratic governors, in particular, have had to face opposition party control of one or both houses. It is easy to cite examples of divided government, for it has existed in such states as New York, New Jersey, Illinois, and Michigan. It is harder to establish a statistical correlation between malapportionment and divided government in two-party states. Malapportionment may seriously affect party balance without causing divided government. The Democrats in Rhode Island, for example, have often been strong enough to win a senatorial majority despite serious underrepresentation of the large cities in that body. On the other hand, malapportionment may handicap a minority party, as has been the case of the Republicans in Kentucky and Maryland. It is also true that factors other than malapportionment may contribute to divided government. When a party that has been in the minority for a long period finally elects a governor, it is unlikely to win a legislative majority because of its failure to recruit a full slate of candidates, or at least of strong candidates, and perhaps because of the voters' unwillingness to make a complete break with previous voting habits. In some states one party has so much of its electoral support concentrated in a few populous counties, and the remainder is so thinly distributed, that the party is unable to translate a popular majority into a legislative majority. Gerrymandering and the use of multi-member districts may either exaggerate or counteract the effect of malapportionment on party representation in the legislature. Midterm elections may be another cause of divided government.

It is probably more meaningful to measure the relationship between malapportionment and partisan balance in the legislature than to calculate only the frequency of divided government, and this relationship is clearest in the northeastern–midwestern industrial states. Table 1 in-

TABLE 1. RELATIONSHIP BETWEEN MALAPPORTIONMENT AND PARTY STRENGTH IN LEGISLATURE IN ELEVEN NORTH-EAST AND MIDWEST INDUSTRIAL STATES, 1953–1963 *

State Legislatures	Value of Vote of Largest County Category (Range of States)	Average Difference Between % of Dems. Elected to Legislature and Dem. % of Vote for Governor #		Legislative Sessions				
		Range	Median	Total	R Leg	D Leg	D Gov	R Gov
Sen—Mass., Ohio Hou—N.J., R.I., Mass., Ill.	111–100	+16 to −11	+3	29	5	5	5	5
Sen—Ill., Pa., Wisc., N.Y., Conn. Hou—Mich., Pa., Wisc., N.Y.	93–77	+11 to −35	−6	36	14	0		
Sen—R.I., Mich., Ind., N.J. Hou—Ohio, Ind., Conn.	72–41	−2 to −20	−16	29	15	2		

* Only those legislative elections are included that coincided with gubernatorial elections; therefore, in states with staggered senatorial terms, only those senators are included who were elected at the time of gubernatorial elections. Only legislative sessions immediately following a gubernatorial election are counted, but the partisan makeup of these sessions includes both newly elected and holdover legislators (the latter in the senates).

A plus indicates that the Democratic percentage of legislative seats is higher than the Democratic vote for governor. A minus indicates the Democratic percentage of legislative seats is lower.

dicates that in this area the Democratic Party's strength in the legislature has lagged behind its gubernatorial vote most in those legislative bodies where the apportionment system discriminated most against the metropolitan counties. The Democrats usually had an advantage only in those legislative bodies where metropolitan counties were represented as well as or better than other counties. I have included only those legislative elections held coincidentally with gubernatorial elections and only the first legislative session in a governor's term to eliminate distortions caused by midterm elections.

The effects of malapportionment in years to come cannot be analyzed in isolation from other political trends in the states. For the most part, reapportionment is likely to accelerate these trends. The rural areas of the United States are areas of traditional party loyalties, usually Republican in the North and Democratic in the South. Population trends are eroding these traditional bases of partisan strength, and the effect of reapportionment is to accelerate this process of erosion. In two-party states both parties are forced to develop platforms and find candidates capable of appealing to the metropolitan voter, and this means that the balance of power is changing within each party. Reapportionment assures that this change will be reflected in the legislative parties as well. In the northern industrial states the Democratic Party has been urban–dominated since the New Deal, and in the short run it is likely to benefit from reapportionment. The rural counties that have traditionally provided the Republican base of support are losing population, and that party, to stay alive, must appeal to the urban and particularly the suburban voters. Reapportionment means that Republican legislative parties will become more urban and less rural, with a constituency base approximating that of Republican governors in northern states.

Most of the remaining one-party states are those in the South that have long been dominated by the Democratic Party. The South today is the scene of political ferment: traditional party loyalties are beginning to lose their hold and the Republican Party is beginning to compete seriously for state and local offices. The southern Republican parties have benefited from several developments: the presidential candidacies of Eisenhower, Nixon, and Goldwater, all of whom carried some southern states; the growing domination of the Democratic Party by its northern, metropolitan wing; and the growing salience for the southern voter of the civil rights issue. In most of the recent national and state elections the greatest southern Republican gains have been made in the metropolitan counties.[2] Gradually the Republican Party has begun to run candidates for state legislative offices in the South. The proportion of legislative seats contested by Republican candidates has risen in some recent elections from few or none to one-half or more in Texas, Florida, Alabama, and South Carolina, for example. In most of the southern states (outside of pockets of traditional Republican strength), half to two-thirds of the Republican legislative candidates, and nearly all of the successful ones, have been in metropolitan counties. It is here that the party has the organization, financing, candidates, and potential voters to launch serious campaigns for legislative seats.

The partisan effect of reapportionment in the South is clear: the increase in metropolitan representation means an increase in the number of seats that are potentially Republican. In a few states this effect has already been felt. After the Florida legislature took the first step toward reapportionment, a special election was held in 1963 to fill 28 new House seats in metropolitan counties; the Republicans contested 27 of these seats, won 11 of them, and thereby tripled their representation in the Florida House. The Republican Party in Georgia increased its legislative seats from 4 in 1962 to 32 in 1965. Most of these were in urban counties that had gained in representation.

Another trend that is related to reapportionment is the increasing political power of the Negro. Northern Negro voters are concentrated in metropolitan centers. In the South it appears likely that Negro voters in the large cities will become a more important political force than those who live in the rural black belt. The urban Negro will probably face fewer restrictions on the franchise, will be better organized, and will be under more aggressive and skillful leadership. The shift of legislative seats from rural to metropolitan counties increases the potential influence of the Negro in state legislatures. It is noteworthy that nine of the ten Negroes elected in the 1964 and 1965 legislative elections in Georgia came from Fulton County (Atlanta), which increased its legislative seats from 10 to 31 between 1962 and 1965. The effect of reapportionment on Negro legislative power cannot be measured only in terms of the number of Negroes elected to the legislature. In any legislative district having a substantial proportion of Negro voters, we can expect that Negroes—particularly if organized and articulate—will have effective access to the legislature.

Metropolitan Districting

As a result of reapportionment the metropolitan counties in an increasing number of states will be able to elect

THE CHANGING POLITICAL ENVIRONMENT

a majority of legislators as well as to cast a majority of the vote in statewide elections. But there is no reason to believe that the legislators, any more than the voters, will vote with unanimity. As the metropolitan areas grow in size, they grow in diversity, and these diverse interests make a variety of demands on government, demands that often conflict in purpose or at least in priority. How the legislature handles these demands depends in part on the legislative strength of each of these interests, and this in turn is affected by the system of districting used for metropolitan counties. The long conflict over the apportionment of seats between urban and rural counties has been settled, but little attention has been given to methods of districting and to the representation of interests within metropolitan counties. In those large counties that elected only one or a few legislators, districting has only recently become a problem.

One method of districting is to divide metropolitan counties into single-member districts. Another method is to elect all legislators at-large within the county. A third is to divide the county into several multi-member districts, each usually electing two to four members. In 1961 two-thirds of the senators in multi-member counties were chosen in a single-member districts and one-third in multi-member countywide districts; a little more than one-third of the representatives were elected by each method, and the remainder came from multi-member districts smaller than an entire county.[3] Countywide at-large elections were used for House members in most of the metropolitan counties in southern states.

The greater the size and diversity of a county, the greater will be the differences in the effects of single and multi-member districts. When a great many legislators are elected at large, the voters may be confronted with long lists of candidates. Twenty-five to forty candidates were common before reapportionment in the primary elections in Jefferson County, Alabama, and Davidson County, Tennessee. In general elections the long list of candidates encourages the voter to cast a straight-ticket ballot. Reapportionment has increased the voter's burden, and this seems to have been an important reason why several states have abandoned countywide legislative elections when adopting new apportionments. It is more expensive for candidates to run countywide campaigns, and increased expenses mean that candidates must rely more heavily on party organizations or interest groups to win elections.

Countywide at-large elections benefit the majority party in a county. Because straight-ticket voting is common, one party is likely to elect a full slate of candidates unless the parties are almost even in voting support or unless individual candidates are unusually popular. A recent survey of elections in the multi-member districts of Indiana, Michigan, Pennsylvania, and West Virginia showed that of 338 county delegations elected, only 13 contained both Democrats and Republicans. Single-member districts also discriminate against the minority party, but to a lesser extent. The proportion of single-member districts that a minority party can win will depend on how much gerrymandering occurs and on the extent to which that party's voting strength is concentrated in a few parts of the county.

The method of districting that is adopted in a metropolitan county affects more than partisan interests, however. Ethnic minorities, such as Negroes, are more likely to have a stronger voice in the legislature if single-member districts are used; but the way in which these district lines are drawn may affect the ability of such minorities to elect legislators who are responsive to their interests. The term "racial gerrymandering" is sometimes used to describe districting that spreads Negro voting strength among several districts, but there is an important difference between the partisan and ethnic effects of districting. If a party's voting strength is so scattered among districts that it cannot elect legislators, its votes are wasted. But a minority group may have some influence over a legislator if it has a substantial proportion of voters—and not necessarily a majority—in a district. On the other hand a minority group (like a party) might minimize its effectiveness if its strength were concentrated, and thereby isolated, in just a few districts. The way in which district lines are drawn clearly affects the ability of various interests to influence legislators, but the effect is more complex and subtle than might appear on the surface.

The representation of interests in multi-member districts may be affected by the "place" system. This method requires legislative candidates to run for a particular numbered position or place, thus making it unnecessary for every candidate to compete against every other candidate. One of the reasons suggested in some southern counties for using the place system is that it eliminates the possibility of "single-shot" voting, a tactic by which members of a group—such as Negroes—cast only a single vote in a multi-member district in an effort to elect an individual candidate. On the other hand, the place system enables a political party or a faction to nominate a balanced slate of candidates, one that is balanced along ethnic or geographic lines, for example.[4]

The racial and partisan implications of districting are

only the most obvious ones. The way in which district lines are drawn affects every interest, and the use of countywide districts leads to the overrepresentation of whatever group may be in the majority—urban or suburban, upper or lower income, white or Negro, liberal or conservative. One reason why it is difficult to predict the effects of reapportionment on policy is that the continuing uncertainty about how metropolitan districting will be handled makes it unclear which metropolitan interests and viewpoints will dominate in the legislature.

In Ohio, after years of partisan controversy over metropolitan districting, single-member districts have replaced countywide districts, as of the 1966 election. One of the effects of the new constitution in Michigan has been to substitute single-member for small multi-member districts in metropolitan counties. Oregon continues to divide its largest counties into several multi-member districts but has instituted the place system for legislative elections. The Tennessee legislature abandoned the long-established practice of countywide elections and adopted single-member districts in its metropolitan counties; it specified that it took this step in order to "eliminate long and cumbersome ballots, provide identifiable constituencies for each senator and representative, assure voters . . . of a single senator and representative specifically to represent them, and minimize the dilution or cancellation of the voting strength of various ethnic, political, economic, or social elements of the population within such counties."[5] The Alabama legislature, on the other hand, adopted a resolution opposing the division of counties into districts because this would lead to "sectionalism and bossism," such as characterized ward elections in large cities. In Georgia, both the racial and the partisan implications of metropolitan districting have been debated in the legislative halls and in the courts. The legislature has adopted plans for electing some metropolitan legislators at large and some from single-member districts. In Florida, the question of districting in metropolitan counties is a controversial one. The supporters of at-large elections, who have been so far successful in maintaining this system, have argued that it is essential to preserve the metropolitan government that is used in Dade County (Miami). Although there is a trend toward abandonment of county-wide legislative elections in the states, we can expect the controversy to be a continuing one because it affects so many important interests in a variety of ways.

Reapportionment and Legislative Policies

In recent years there has been a debate among political scientists about whether massive reapportionment in the states will bring about significant changes in policy. Malapportionment has affected the legislative strength of parties in the past, at least for the northeastern and midwestern states, and reapportionment can be expected to affect the legislative power of parties and other interests. But, if malapportionment has not affected policy outputs in the past, reapportionment might not be expected to have policy consequences in the future. Several recent studies have sought to determine whether "the policy choices of malapportioned legislatures are noticeably different from the policy choices of well-apportioned legislatures" and whether "these differences in policies can be traced to malapportionment rather than some other condition."[7] The technique has been to calculate interstate correlations between indexes of malapportionment and output variables such as levels of spending for education and welfare, several aspects of the tax structure, and a few other types of legislation.

There are a number of technical problems in trying to make such calculations. The index of malapportionment most widely used in these studies is the Schubert–Press index, which is a complex measure of the deviation of an apportionment from an ideal but does not directly measure metropolitan underrepresentation.[8] The David–Eisenberg index measures the value of the vote in the largest population category of counties in a state.[9] Although the size of the largest counties varies from state to state (with not every state having any counties of over half-million population), the David–Eisenberg index does provide the only direct index of urban underrepresentation as well as the only index that has been shown to have any significant correlation with a few policy outputs. Every apportionment index is an average of the index derived for the Senate and that for the House (although the Schubert–Press index gives greater weight to the Senate.) The average index of malapportionment may be the same for two states even though in one state metropolitan counties are moderately underrepresented in both houses and in the other these counties are equitably represented in one house and seriously underrepresented in the other. In which state would we expect malapportionment to have the greatest effect on policy outputs? Because legislation must pass both houses, it might be argued that an apportionment index based on the legislative branch in which the metropolitan counties were more underrepresented would be the best one to use in measuring correlations with policy outputs. But whatever index of apportionment is used, it is important to realize that it can provide only a rough estimate of metropolitan representation in the legislature.

The measurement of legislative output is as difficult as devising an appropriate index of urban underrepresentation. Most studies of the effects of apportionment rely heavily on the levels of state spending for education and welfare. The major disadvantage of measuring state spending is that it is more closely related to variations in the wealth of states than are most other measures. Moreover, some spending programs are adopted in response to federal programs that require matching funds from the states. Some studies measure what might be called the symptoms of state spending, such as the high school drop-out rate and the percentage of selective service examinees who failed the mental test, but these are so indirectly related to specific legislation that we would not expect them to vary precisely with the extent of malapportionment from state to state. Anyone who tries to select specific policy outputs from the vast amount of legislation passed in the states is forced to make arbitrary judgments, and he may easily fail to isolate those output variables that are most likely to have been affected by malapportionment.

The conclusions of most of the recent studies concerning malapportionment and policy outputs can be summarized in the words of Thomas Dye:

> On the whole, the policy choices of malapportioned legislatures are not noticeably different from the policy choices of well-apportioned legislatures. Most of the policy differences which do occur turn out to be a product of socio-economic differences among the states rather than a direct product of apportionment

practices. Relationships that appear between
malapportionment and public policy are so slight
that reapportionment is not likely to bring about any
significant policy changes.[10]

It is apparent from these and other studies that there is
a strong positive relationship between the wealth of a
state, its urbanization, and its industrialization on the
one hand and its policy outputs. The wealthier urban–
industrial states spend more and tend to adopt more
"liberal" programs. There are two principal reasons for
this. The wealthier states (however poorly apportioned)
have far greater resources to spend on state programs
than do the impoverished states (however well apportioned). In 1963, for example, the per capita income was
more than twice as high in New York, Connecticut,
Illinois, and California as it was in Mississippi. Moreover,
it is in these states where the greatest proportion of the
population is concentrated in metropolitan counties, and
where we would expect the political strength of metropolitan interests to be greatest. When we ask whether
policy outputs vary with the degree of malapportionment,
we are, in a sense, asking the wrong question. Why should
we expect a well-apportioned legislature in an overwhelmingly rural state to pass more liberal legislation
or adopt larger budgets than a poorly apportioned legislature in an overwhelmingly urban state? It is the proportion of metropolitan members in the legislature, not the
value of the vote in metropolitan counties, that ought to
affect policy outputs.

We should not expect, therefore, to find that simple
correlations between any standard index of malapportionment and particular policy outputs are high. One way of

controlling the level of urbanization, as well as wealth, in
interstate comparisons is to use partial correlations, as
some of the studies have done. It was the use of partial
correlations that enabled Dye to conclude that socio-
economic differences among the states affected policy outputs more than apportionment practices did. But there is
no reason why we should expect apportionment practices,
in the abstract, to affect policy, and no reason to be sur-
prised that urbanization has greater explanatory power.
When the technique of interstate correlations is used, the
contrasts among the states in wealth and urbanization are
so great as to obscure whatever effect malapportionment
has. If we rank the states according to the percent of
population living in counties of over 100,000 and according to the proportion of legislative seats apportioned
to this group of counties (averaging the proportions in the
two houses) we get a Spearman rank order correlation of
.91. Consequently, if we attempt to relate policy outputs
to metropolitan political strength by using a rank order
correlation, it will be difficult to isolate the effect of
malapportionment on metropolitan political power and on
policy outputs. The interstate indexes of apportionment
and the measures of policy outputs are too crude to isolate
the impact of apportionment on policy.

Another difficulty with interstate correlations is that we
cannot assume that equal degrees of malapportionment
would have the same effect in different states. The effect
of malapportionment might be greatest in those states
where it would relegate metropolitan counties having a
majority of the population to a minority status in the
legislature. Certainly the effects of equal degrees of
apportionment are likely to be different in heavily metropolitan and industrial states and in overwhelmingly

rural states. One final difficulty in any attempt to measure the effects of malapportionment precisely is that there are very few states, urban or rural, that have not been malapportioned to some degree.

One type of policy output that is often said to be affected by apportionment is the proportion of state aid going to local governments in metropolitan and rural counties. In certain states there have been examples of proportionately much greater state aid to rural counties. In Florida, for example, each county received an equal share of state race-track revenue that was returned to the counties; the annual per capita amount one year was only twenty cents in Dade County and over $61.00 in one of the smallest counties.[11] This is one type of policy output that may be minimally affected by the levels of wealth in states. We can calculate the extent to which counties get the state aid they "deserve" by dividing the percentage of state aid going to each county by the percentage of state population living in that county. If we look at all counties having at least 100,000 population as a group in each state, we can rank the forty-two states that have such counties according to the percentage of "deserved" aid received by local governments in this category of counties and compare it to the proportion of legislative seats held by these counties (averaging the percentages in the two houses). The resulting Spearman rank order correlation of .72 demonstrates that local governments in metropolitan counties are apt to get a larger share of state aid (compared to their population) in states where they have more legislative power. But if we compare deserved aid to the percentage of the state population living in these counties we also get a rank order correlation of .72. (It will be recalled that there was a correlation of .91 between the percentage of population of these counties and their percentage of legislative seats.) It is possible to conclude that in the more urbanized states the local governments in metropolitan counties are likely to get an amount of state aid that is closer to what they deserve—in some cases because of their general political power, and in some cases because of their specific power in the legislature.

Perhaps the fundamental difficulty in trying to measure the consequences of malapportionment in the past by interstate comparisons is that in few if any of the states have the metropolitan counties been both equitably and powerfully represented in the legislature. In roughly half of the states the metropolitan residents have constituted less than half of the total population; even in the few states where they were equitably represented, they were outnumbered in the legislature. In the remaining states, particularly in the industrial North, the legislature was unlikely to be fully responsive to metropolitan needs because: (1) the largest counties were usually underrepresented in one or both houses; (2) the metropolitan counties usually elected Democratic legislators, but that party in most states held a minority position in the legislature until very recent years; (3) the quality of metropolitan representation has been poor, metropolitan party organizations having used legislative nominations as a form of patronage to reward the faithful party workers. It can be argued, I think with considerable validity, that the effects of malapportionment on policy outputs can be best evaluated, not by measuring differences among states with different degrees of malapportionment but by studying the response of state legislatures as a whole to the challenges of the metropolis.

Roscoe C. Martin, in his recent book *The Cities and the*

Federal System, eloquently describes the response, or nonresponse, of the states. From 1942 to 1962 the proportion of state revenues going to local government declined gradually. Almost two-thirds of this aid has gone for education, and most of the rest has been for public welfare and highways. While state assistance in these traditional fields is substantial and widely accepted, the states have been reluctant to assume any financial responsibility for problems of special concern to the cities. Moreover, the costs of traditional state programs have been rising rapidly in recent years. In 1962 less than 2.0 percent of state aid to localities was directed toward public housing, urban renewal, urban planning, airports, and similar urban needs, and nothing was spent on mass transit.[12]

> The single overwhelming conclusion to be drawn from this analysis is that the states' concern for the vast new problems of metropolitan America, as measured by monetary contributions toward their alleviation, is quite casual. There is little evidence, indeed, that the states recognize these problems as anything more than very limited state responsibilities.[13]

Martin believes that the traditional services performed by the state are ones that could serve statewide needs in a largely agrarian society. Because the states are not yet totally urban, assistance to urban and particularly metropolitan areas "takes on the character of helping to meet specialized needs of individual places as identified by special groups." Martin concludes that "the vast new problems of urban America are unique in the experience of the states, which react to them in an impatient and sometimes a truculent manner. Nothing would please the

states more than for the cities and their problems to de-
materialize into thin air." [14]

A New Political Climate

The cities and their problems are not going to dis-
appear; instead they are going to become the principal
concern of most state governments, as well as a major
concern of the federal government. During the last three
decades the federal government has been playing an
increasingly active part in metropolitan problems. Since a
larger proportion of federal grants are made directly to
cities, fears are often expressed that the states are being
by-passed. There is no reason to expect that federal
contributions to metropolitan programs will decline. The
states and cities alone cannot bear the financial burdens,
and those urban interests that are seeking new and expanded programs will use their political power in Washington to demand increasing federal participation. As the
federal government continues to bear a large share of the
costs, it will continue to determine priorities and to set
standards to which state and local authorities must conform.

The principal reason why the state will be unable to
leave metropolitan problems to the federal and local
government is that metropolitan political interests will
demand state participation. The state has the statutory
power to deal with metropolitan problems, and the state
alone has the authority to streamline the governmental
and tax structure within the metropolis. The state has the
authority to overrule decisions of local government, to
give and take away local taxing authority, to mediate the
differences between local governments. Conflicts over tax-

ation, annexation, planning, and other issues between various local governments and the interests that dominate each are likely to be resolved at the state level. The state has a tax structure that can be expanded to produce more revenue if there is sufficient political pressure for such an expansion. When the federal government cuts back on aid to the states and localities because of its international commitments or anti-inflationary fiscal policies, there will be pressure on state governments to take up the slack. Because federal funds will never be sufficient to satisfy even the most urgent metropolitan needs, and because the states cannot give the federal government complete control over setting priorities, state governments will be forced to bear more of the financial responsibility for meeting metropolitan needs.

The political interests located in the metropolis will make demands on state government that are too loud and too persistent to be denied. When there is approximate consensus among these groups, they will dominate the decision-making process in most state governments. When these groups are in disagreement, they will increasingly turn to the state government for the resolution of their conflicts. In 1960 there were twenty-two states in which a majority of the population lived in counties of over 100,000, and these states contained two-thirds of the nation's population. By 1970 the proportion of states that are predominantly urban will obviously increase.

The massive reapportionment of the 1960's has guaranteed that the metropolitan counties will be able to elect a legislative majority, as well as a governor, in a large and increasing number of the states; but reapportionment does not predetermine the political alliances that will emerge in the metropolitan–dominated states. One of the elements of uncertainty, already discussed, concerns the form that legislative districting will take in metropolitan counties. Another uncertain factor is the way in which the political parties will react to metropolitan change.

In the northern industrial states, the Democratic Party has been essentially urban and the Republican Party rural. Because of districting, each of the legislative parties has been even more homogeneous in its constituent base, and for this reason the legislative parties have been relatively cohesive in voting on major socio-economic issues. Democratic legislators have represented urban districts with average and below-average levels of income, and some of them have been responsive to the discipline of urban political organizations. As the metropolitan constituencies grow more diverse, the Democratic Party may not be able to retain this level of unity. The interests of Negro and low-income constituents in the central cities will clash with those of the suburbanites when the legislature debates such issues as housing, education, and levels of taxation and spending. It is not yet clear how articulate and politically effective the Negro and white low-income voters will become, but it is increasingly clear that their demands—whether expressed through political organizations or in demonstrations and riots in the streets—cannot be ignored. It is also clear that some of the sharpest conflicts of interest are between whites and Negroes in the low-income sections of the city. The Democratic Party must represent diversified interests in the metropolis; it cannot win elections by gaining only the votes of the poor or only suburban support. Many of the conflicts over metropolitan policies will be fought out within the Democratic Party, and in northern states that party is unlikely to remain as united and disciplined as it has been in the past.

Most of the Republicans who have been able to win governorships in northern industrial states in recent years have been men such as Nelson Rockefeller, George Romney, and William Scranton, who are sensitive to metropolitan needs. Most of them have had to deal with Republican legislative parties that were still dominated by rural members. Reapportionment has made it both possible and necessary for the Republican Party to compete for metropolitan legislative seats, particularly in the higher income suburban areas. The Republican legislative parties are likely to become increasingly heterogeneous and disunified because of the sharp differences between the interests of high-income suburban and low-income rural constituencies. It would not be accurate to label these as "liberal" and "conservative" wings. The suburban Republican legislator may represent a constituency that is conservative in many respects and resists the demands of urban (central–city) constituencies, but the suburban voters will be disposed to make positive demands on government in such fields as education, planning, and mass transit. The Republican Party in northern states, no less than the Democratic Party, faces the problem of redefining or rediscovering its constituency base.

It is more difficult to generalize about political trends in southern states. Florida and Texas are predominantly metropolitan, Mississippi and Arkansas are overwhelmingly rural, and the rest of the states are scattered in between these extremes. Racial conflicts are still salient enough for the voters in some of these states to obscure all other issues, and in the years immediately ahead this fact will largely determine partisan tactics in such states. Negro voters are a better organized and more potent force in some southern states than in the others. Throughout the South it is probably true that party loyalties are less firmly held and are less predictive of political behavior than they are in the North.

In the more urbanized states, such as Florida and Texas, the Republican Party has the best opportunity to build a strong base in the metropolitan counties, particularly in the areas of above-average income. This base may be firm enough to give Republicans a strong and relatively cohesive legislative party within a few years. In the less urbanized states the Republican Party is also likely to win gubernatorial votes and elect legislators in the high-income areas of metropolitan counties. But this support will not be enough to win a majority, and in such states the Republican Party may try to win greater support in the rural counties also. In such states as Kentucky, Tennessee, Virginia, and North Carolina the Republican Party already has a traditional base of support in the mountain counties. In the Deep South, Republicans may be able to use the racial issue to win rural votes, though this possibility is largely dependent on the course taken by the Democratic Party.

The Democratic Party in southern states, long dominated by conservative, rural whites, is going to be a battleground in the years ahead. In the more urbanized states we shall probably see replications of the liberal–conservative split that has characterized the Democratic Party in Texas. Negro groups are likely to play an important part in a fragile liberal coalition. If the Republican Party succeeds in winning high-income voters in the metropolis, the conservative wing of the Democratic

Party may be relegated to the rural areas, with their constantly declining populations. Although the long-run trends in Texas point to a party realignment that would pit a liberal Democratic Party against a conservative Republican Party, events of the last few years in that state suggest that such an outcome is neither an immediate nor yet an inevitable prospect for the more urbanized states. In the less urbanized states the Democratic Party has three constituencies today: the rural white voters, the low-income urban whites, and the Negroes. Their interests are in conflict, and these conflicts seem to be growing rather than declining in intensity. One has only to look at the events of 1966 in Arkansas, Alabama, and Georgia to realize that the Democratic Party is in a state of chaos and may be unable to retain the support of all these groups. Although, in the long run, southern politics will become increasingly focused around metropolitan issues, the outline of this new metropolitan politics is still obscured today by the smoke that arises from the politics of racial conflict.

III

The Changing Face of
State Legislatures

Malcolm E. Jewell

STATE LEGISLATURES TODAY HAVE EMERGED
from obscurity into the spotlight of professional and
public attention. Political scientists are analyzing them
with greater care and sophistication, foundations are sup-
porting efforts to study and improve them, the press is
scrutinizing them more critically, and citizens' groups are
trying to reform them. Except for some of the political
scientists, those who have taken an interest in the legislatures are principally interested in reform. The main thrust
of reform proposals has been well summarized in a recent
report, from the American Assembly, on state legislatures
in American politics:

> State legislatures have failed to meet the challenge of
> change because they have been handicapped by re-
> stricted powers, inadequate tools and facilities, ineffi-
> cient organization and procedures, unattractive fea-
> tures that produce excessive turnover in legislative
> service and lack of public understanding and con-

fidence and because legislatures themselves have been unduly timid in using the powers already in their possession to strengthen their role.[1]

The specific reforms that are being proposed are not radical. Indeed they are patterned on the steps that have already been taken in a few of the large industrial states, where the problems faced by state government are most complex and the need for legislative competence and efficiency is most obvious. The reformers propose that the legislature should be more professional. Legislators should be better paid and should serve longer terms, and they should have better staff assistance, professional advice, and facilities for working. The legislature should meet more often for longer sessions, and it should be better organized to permit both more efficiency and more careful deliberation.

It is impossible to predict how widely or rapidly these reforms will be adopted, but it is reasonable to suggest that such proposals indicate the direction of change to be anticipated in the years ahead. As states become more industrialized, and as state governments are forced to grapple more often with the complex problems of the metropolis, the legislatures will have to work more consistently and more skillfully. Because this is the continuation of a trend that has been under way for some years, it should be possible to speculate—without the aid of a crystal ball—about the consequences of these changes for state government as a whole.

Even while planned reforms are under way, the legislature is being exposed to the unplanned consequences of political change. The massive reapportionment of legislative seats and changes in the character of state party competition are beginning to affect the legislature in many ways, including the recruitment, caliber, and tenure of members and the organization of power within the legislature. Because many of these changes are of recent origin, it is more difficult to predict what their consequences will be, but it is useful to explore the possibilities. There is no certainty that these political trends will complement the effort to make the legislature more professional; in some respects the consequences of planned and unplanned change seem to be contradictory.

Because it is impossible to isolate the effects of reform from the tides of political change, we must look at their combined effects if we are to understand and anticipate the trends of today and tomorrow. To ignore the political implications of reform would be unrealistic. The legislature cannot be given increased competence and better tools without affecting the ways in which these will be employed. Though the consequences of reform cannot always be foreseen, the interrelationships within the legislative system are so complex that changes in one part will obviously affect many of the others, perhaps in ways that are unintended. Just as it is unrealistic to think that reform can be carried out in a political vacuum, it is naïve to believe that reforms will not have political consequences. The underlying philosophy of legislative reform—the belief that the legislature should be a more effective and powerful participant in the process of government—is political. It is rooted, more fundamentally, in a belief about the future of the federal system: the state will not wither away; it has the resources, authority, and ability to make a contribution—

along with the federal and local governments—to the solution of metropolitan problems.

The Trend toward a More Professional Legislature

One of the objectives of the reform movement is to attract better qualified men to legislative office and to encourage them to stay in office in order to develop competence and gain experience. The American Assembly, while recognizing that "turnover in office in a representative assembly is inevitable," expressed concern about "well qualified legislators who voluntarily drop out from service because of the frustrations of legislative life." [2] The remedies usually proposed are: longer terms, to cut down the burdens of frequent campaigns; higher salaries, to attract more qualified men and make it possible for them to serve for prolonged periods without financial sacrifice; and assistance and facilities, to make legislative service more professional and less frustrating. In recent years a number of states have taken steps toward more professional legislatures. Between 1947 and 1965 the number of states using an annual or biennial salary, rather than per diem pay, increased from 26 to 34. Particularly in some of the larger states, salaries have been raised substantially. California increased its biennial salary from $2,400 to $12,000, New York from $5,000 to $20,000, New Jersey from $1,000 to $15,000, and Michigan from $7.50 a day to $20,000 in a biennium. [3]

In the postwar period there has been very little change in the number of states having four-year terms for either senators or representatives. In only a few of the states have legislators been provided with even a minimum amount of office space and secretarial help. The new legislative building in North Carolina, for example, includes a small office for each member, and there is also a pool of typists. California provides not only secretarial help and office space but an allowance enabling each member to rent and staff an office in his district.

It seems probable that higher salaries and better facilities, in specific cases, encourage qualified men to run and to seek re-election. It is certainly not hard to find examples of individuals who have left the legislature in part because the costs of continued service were too high. But there is no evidence to show whether the generally higher salaries, and the additional benefits in a few states, have attracted substantially more qualified legislators, nor would it be easy to reach an objective conclusion on this point. There is some evidence of declining turnover in state legislatures. In ten states for which data are available the proportion of legislators who were serving their first term was about one-third in the 1925–35 period, and only about one-fifth in a sample of sessions between 1950 and 1963. But there is no direct evidence that this decline was a result of salary increases or that legislators who are serving for longer periods are the more qualified ones.

Reapportionment and changes in party competition will also have an effect on recruitment and turnover that is just as important as, if less predictable than, the effects of better salaries and facilities. There will be fewer rural legislators, a temporary increase in urban legislators, and a continuing increase in those elected from the suburbs. What factors affect recruitment and tenure in each type of district? In the absence of comprehensive studies, we can only suggest a few possibilities based on fragments of research. Data from primary elections in five southern states (Alabama, Florida, North Carolina, South Carolina, and Texas) over a period of several years indicate that in each state a larger proportion of incumbents seek renomination in nonmetropolitan districts (77 percent in the median state) than in metropolitan districts (67 percent in the median state).[4] It is obvious that no single pattern of recruitment and tenure can be described as typical of rural legislators. In some small counties there is little competition for the office, and a member who enjoys legislative service may remain entrenched in office indefinitely. At the other extreme is the individual, often retired or semi-retired, who is persuaded to serve one or two terms as a "civic duty" but has no interest in a legislative career. Barber, in his study of Connecticut legislators, found that members elected from the small towns tended to be either "spectators," who were looking forward to many years of service, or "reluctants," who had consented to run for only a brief term.[5]

In multi-county districts of some states, particularly in the South, it has been common for the legislative seat to be rotated among the various counties. This practice limits a member to one or two consecutive terms and thus reduces the proportion of experienced legislators. Reapportionment is likely to make rotation impractical in most senatorial districts by increasing the number of counties per district to more than two or three. At the same time reapportionment may encourage rotation in House districts containing counties that no longer have a representative of their own.

As an increasing proportion of legislators is elected from metropolitan counties, it becomes more important to discover what factors in these areas motivate men to run for office. In some of the larger cities, where political machines have remained effective, legislative nominations have been awarded to men who have served the party faithfully. This form of patronage was possibly less valuable and attractive because it did not pay as much as a full-time appointive job. Men who have been recruited in this fashion have often remained in the legislature for prolonged periods—if they continued to serve the party and to vote in accord with whatever instructions were given. The shift of seats within the metropolitan counties to the suburbs and the decline of organizational effectiveness will make this pattern of recruitment and tenure less common. A second type of legislator, whom Barber calls the "advertiser," is common in metropolitan counties. Part of his motivation in seeking legislative office is the hope that the publicity he gets and the contacts he makes will enhance his business interests. Such persons usually do not view legislative service as a long-term career, and it is possible that they will be less attracted to legislative service as longer and more frequent sessions make it more time-consuming and reduce the time that they can devote to business interests.[6]

Barber found another type of legislator to be common in the large cities, and this type he named the "lawmaker": the legislator who plays an active role in the legislature and is committed to a political career. Barber's "lawmaker" is the "professional" whom the reformers hope to recruit by making a legislative career more attractive. It is not clear how many states can afford full-time legislators, how many will be willing to raise the salary to the level where legislators can depend on it as their principal source of income. At present only nine states pay at least $5,000 a year, and only Michigan and New York pay at least $10,000. As the length and frequency of legislative sessions increase to the point that legislative service becomes almost a full-time job in some states, it is questionable how many capable and successful business and professional men will be willing to neglect their work and concentrate on legislative careers.

If it is uncertain whether reapportionment will increase or decrease the proportion of members with an interest in long-term careers, it is probable that the shift of seats to metropolitan counties will subject legislators to greater competition when they seek renomination and re-election. Studies in several northern states have demonstrated that there is more primary competition in metropolitan than in nonmetropolitan counties. A study of legislative primaries in five southern states shows that incumbents are more apt to face opposition in the primary in metropolitan than in nonmetropolitan districts; however, the incumbents who run in metropolitan counties are slightly less likely to be beaten in the primary. This study also suggests, however, that legislative primary competition is affected by several factors other than the urban–rural one. The level of competition varies more from state to state than it does between metropolitan and rural districts within some states. Among the southern rural districts, the level of primary competition is sharply reduced in the black-belt counties.[7]

We can predict with greater assurance the effects of reapportionment on the frequency of close two-party competition for legislative seats. Most rural districts are solidly enough controlled by one party so that an incumbent legislator faces little chance of being defeated once he has won renomination. But the level of two-party competition varies substantially among urban counties. Many of the districts in the central cities of metropolitan areas are solidly Democratic, but it is these areas that usually have stagnant or declining populations. The suburban sections of metropolitan counties, which will be the continuing beneficiaries of reapportionment, usually do not have traditional loyalties to either party. It is in these districts that the level of party competition is, and can be expected to remain, high. The proportion of closely competitive seats (in a partisan sense) in most state legislatures has been low. This has been true even in a state like Michigan, which has been closely competitive in statewide elections, but had partisan turnover in only 10 percent of its seats in five elections. One almost certain consequence of reapportionment will be to increase the proportion of legislators who will have to overcome a serious challenge by a partisan opponent in order to win re-election. The obvious consequence of more extensive two-party competition could be to increase turnover and to reduce the level of experience in the legislature.

Congressional incumbents, even in competitive districts, usually have an advantage over their opponents because they are better known to the constituents, and the veteran congressman often becomes so well known and is able to accomplish so much for his constituents—by patient attention to small favors—that he is virtually unbeatable. Is it likely that veteran legislators who devote most of their time to their job will be able to achieve a similar degree of security against defeat at the polls? Can an experienced legislator in a large metropolitan area achieve as much visibility as a congressman, can he capture attention in the headlines (in competition with other legislators in the area), and can he overcome the handicap of not having the lifelong, firsthand acquaintance with most of his constituents that rural legislators have so often enjoyed? These are questions that remain to be answered, and the answers will help to determine whether the price of increasing two-party competition in legislative elections will be an increase in turnover and a lowering of the level of experience in the legislature.

The Demand for Greater Legislative Competence

A major objective of those who seek reform is to give the legislature greater competence to deal with the complex problems that confront the states. There is widespread belief that, in the words of the American Assembly, "legislatures should be continuing bodies meeting in annual plenary sessions, without limitation of time or subject." [8] Even those who prefer time limits would generally agree that the legislature needs more than sixty or ninety days to do its work and that its committees should be free to work between sessions. If severe limits are placed on the length of sessions, the legislature lacks the time for adequate hearings and careful study, and the climax of its session is inevitably chaotic. Since 1947 the number of states holding regular annual sessions has increased from six to twenty, but the proportion that limit the length of sessions to ninety days or less has remained about one-half.

Legislative councils and interim committees have become increasingly active in the states. They provide a vehicle for conducting research, holding hearings, and analyzing proposed legislation between the regular legislative sessions. The success of the legislative council is largely dependent on the quantity and quality of the staff available to it. In many states most of the professional staff members are assigned to the legislative council; in some cases individual committees, particularly those dealing with the budget, have year-round staff assistance. Although a comprehensive description of the scope of legislative staffing is not available, we may estimate it roughly from data on the budgets of legislative councils. In 1947 there were twenty legislative councils for which budget totals were available, and seventeen of these had budgets of $50,000 or less for the biennium. In 1965 there were forty-three legislative councils; fourteen had budgets of over $250,000, and all but five had budgets of over $100,000 for the biennium. Some of the states that rely on interim committees, rather than councils, provide them with adequate staffing. The annual budget for such committees exceeds $2 million in New York and $1 million in California, and California has inaugurated a program of providing professional staff and consultants for all of its substantive standing committees.[9]

The proponents of legislative reform give the highest priority to adequate staffing for the legislative council, as well as for party leadership and the most important committees, and to such services as bill drafting, law revision, and library and reference services. These are perceived not merely as conveniences but as prerequisites to legislative competence. According to the participants in the American Assembly: "By providing these staffs the legislative branch will improve its ability to develop programs, undertake research, exercise oversight, analyze and evaluate the executive budget, insure effective post-audit, and interpret and communicate its activities."[10]

Increasingly, legislative leaders recognize the need for better staffs. One of the most articulate of today's legislative leaders, Speaker Jesse Unruh of the California House, has repeatedly warned that the legislature must be more adequately staffed if it is to avoid being dominated by the executive branch. Unruh has said that adequate staffing is necessary to enable committees "to take an independent view of the executive department's programs, and to put them in a position to offer alternative recommendations to the Legislature ... and to provide continuing and effective program review and oversight of programs approved by the Legislature." [11] With regard to staffing, the state legislatures are in a position comparable to that of the United States Congress twenty years ago. The authors of the 1946 Legislative Reorganization Act, and the members of the joint committee whose study made that legislation possible were convinced that Congress was in danger of being dominated by the President and the executive branch. They believed that Congress needed staff assistance in order to be able to make independent judgments about the legislative proposals being proposed by the Executive. The 1946 Act streamlined the committee structure and authorized adequate staffing for each committee so that it would no longer be necessary for committees to borrow staff personnel from executive agencies. Most state legislators and most legislative committees today lack the time, the information, and the staff assistance to make careful, independent judgments about the bills proposed by the governor and about the budget. If the legislature cannot make independent judgments, it must become a "rubber stamp"; it must follow the lead of someone else, and frequently the most powerful leader available is the governor.

It is important to emphasize that the demand for better staffing and the broader issue of increasing legislative competence are not merely questions of reform; they are questions of power. If we increase the legislature's competence and provide it with better tools, we are equipping it to challenge the executive branch and to demand a larger share of authority for making policy. Not every student of state government would agree that it is desirable to tip the balance of power between the executive and the legislature in the direction of the legislature. The differences of opinion might result both from different philosophies of government and from the interstate variations that now exist in legislative–executive relations. In some states today the governor dominates the legislature and his major proposals are usually adopted with a minimum of deliberation and opposition. In another category of states the legislature seems to pay little attention to the governor's requests, which are neither numerous nor forceful. A third category of states are those in which the governor makes frequent recommendations and works vigorously for their enactment, but the legislature often revises or opposes his requests. It is not very meaningful to discuss legislative–executive relationships in a vacuum. We need to be aware of the interstate variations in practice, and of the political factors that contribute to these variations.

The governor is most likely to dominate the legislature in a one-party state, such as Tennessee or Alabama. If he has constitutional and statutory authority over the most important executive agencies, if he has extensive patronage resources and uses them skillfully, and if his predecessors have accustomed the public to a strong gubernatorial role, the governor is in a powerful position to exercise legislative leadership. Under these circumstances the absence of two-party competition means the absence of an organized legislative minority having the ability and the responsibility to question, amend, and oppose the governor's recommendations.

Some of the weakest governors are also found in states that are dominated by a single party or that have a weak two-party system. These are usually (but not always) rural states in which the governor has been under less pressure to make forceful legislative demands. In some of these states there is strong leadership by a clique or faction within the legislature, as in South Carolina or Florida. Often the governor lacks constitutional and statutory authority over major state agencies; these are run by elected heads or by boards whose members are appointed at staggered times for fixed terms. The governor may have less influence in the legislature than the individual agency leaders who have established independent alliances with powerful legislators.

Many of the major industrial–urban states fit into a third category. These are states with two strong, closely competitive parties. The governor, responding to pressures for new programs and expanded budgets, sends a comprehensive program to the legislature and uses the full weight of his office in an effort to have it enacted. Often the legislators belonging to his party support most of his program, though this varies with personalities, issues, and circumstances. The opposition party is well organized, often cohesive, and frequently arrayed against his program; it is also common for the opposition party to command a majority in at least one house of the legislature. In these states, the governor with a partisan majority in both houses may enact most of his program, but even he has to defend it against the sniping of the opposition party. In this group of states it is not accurate to describe the legislature as a rubber stamp, but it may be argued that legislative action or inaction results more often from partisan considerations than from careful, independent deliberation on the merits of the governor's program.

Proposals to make the legislature more competent are, at bottom, proposals to make it more powerful, and they cannot be considered in a political vacuum. As the demands on state government grow, the governor will probably assume greater responsibilities for initiating legislative programs, even in those rural states where he has been relatively passive until now. It is worth noting that, since 1947, eleven states have increased governors' terms of office to four years. An increasing number of governors will probably gain effective authority over most administrative agencies. At the same time, the growth of two-party competition is likely to guarantee a legislative opposition party that will limit the governor's ability to dominate the legislature in most states. In the strong two-party states reapportionment may reduce the frequency of divided government and thereby strengthen the governor, but the parties will probably become less cohesive and disciplined as they begin to represent more heterogeneous interests.

There are political trends visible in the nation that are likely to create greater equilibrium between the governor and the legislature and to reduce the number of situations in which either branch of government dominates the other. In some states these trends will reinforce the campaign for more competent and vigorous legislatures. But more partisanship in the legislature is not identical to—and may even be inconsistent with—the goal of more competence in the legislature. It might be argued that there are two plausible routes to a stronger legislature (vis-à-vis the governor): a stronger party system *or* greater professional competence. The question is not which route will or should be followed, but what results can we anticipate if—as we predict—both routes are followed simultaneously?

Stronger Legislative Committees

Twenty years ago those who were trying to give Congress the competence necessary for it to "stand up" to the President put their faith in the committee system. The path of reform at the state legislative level leads, with equal logic, to a stronger committee system. Specialized committees can appraise the governor's legislative proposals more carefully than the entire legislature can. Similarly there are advantages in using the committee system for oversight of the executive branch. The skills of a professional staff can often be put to best use within a committee structure.

Most legislative committees today fall short of the strong–committee system, for which the congressional committees might be considered a model. Although the number of committees has been steadily declining, more than half of the legislative bodies have more than twenty committees, some of which are probably overworked and some probably unemployed. In most states there is a high degree of turnover on committees, much higher than is necessitated by the high rate of turnover within the legislature as a whole. In many states it is even common for the chairman to be a new member of a committee. The result is that the committees usually fail to develop a nucleus of men with detailed knowledge, gained from experience, concerning the subject over which the committee has jurisdiction. Committee members with such knowledge are likely to have gained it outside the legislature, because of their business, profession, or other interest. Nor does the committee usually have enough continuity to develop well accepted norms. Because the presiding officer can assign bills without regard to rules of committee jurisdiction, there is no certainty that an education committee, for example, will have the opportunity of acting on a major education bill, particularly if the committee has a record of independent action. The committees are frequently under pressure to act quickly on bills, with a minimum of hearings or deliberation.

In contrast to this common pattern of committees, the American Assembly recommends reforms modeled on congressional practice. The committees should be "few in number, with broad well-defined jurisdictions," and bills should be assigned by subject matter. "Committees should meet regularly in open sessions, and in executive sessions when necessary," and should hold hearings. At least the most important committees should have year-round professional staffs and should be adequately housed and equipped.[12]

It seems likely that many of these reforms will be adopted—at least in the larger states—and committees will assume greater importance in the legislature. This seems to be a predictable trend if the legislature meets for longer sessions, the membership has less turnover, and the staff resources are enhanced. It will become less common for a committee to report out major legislation within a day or two of receiving it, as often happens in Kentucky, or to report out any bill if its sponsor requests it, as in the Illinois legislature. The committees will exercise more independent judgment, and their reports will become more significant in the decision-making process.

Although the path of reform leads to stronger committees, the path of intensified two-party competition leads
in another direction. The powerful congressional committees, buttressed by the seniority system, are among the
greatest obstacles to stronger party cohesion. In states like
New Jersey and Connecticut, where the party caucus is
the focus of decision-making, committees are of minimal
importance. It is true, of course, that the political parties
do not take a stand on every issue, and the committee may
have an important decision-making function with regard
to nonpartisan issues (such as has been true in Pennsylvania); but partisan issues are apt to be the most important
ones confronting the legislature.

The desire of reformers to strengthen legislative
competence by revitalizing the committee system will
tend to clash with the demands of party leaders to
centralize authority in those state legislatures—increasing
in number—that have a strongly competitive two-party
system. We cannot predict the outcome of this conflict,
and it is likely to differ from state to state. One strong
possibility is that the seniority will not achieve the importance in legislative committee assignments that it has in
Congress. Even though veteran legislators may more
frequently be retained on a committee in successive sessions, party leaders are unlikely to surrender the authority
to replace those legislators who have become mavericks.
Similarly, the party leadership will continue the practice
of selecting committee chairmen who have demonstrated
loyalty to the party. As a further consequence of a growing two-party system, we can expect to find the minority
party demanding a proportional share of seats on each
committee, a practice that is not generally accepted in
legislatures dominated by one party. Stronger committees

are not necessarily incompatible with strong legislative parties, but a blend of the two ingredients has yet to be worked out in many of the legislatures.

Budgetary Review

Legislatures that are more professional and better staffed and that meet for longer periods and make greater use of committees are prone to supervise state budgets more carefully. At least twenty state legislatures now have joint committees (or committees in one house), equipped with staff, that carry out a continuing study of state revenues and expenses and provide a critical appraisal of the executive budget. Fifteen of the committees have assumed this function, or been staffed for the first time, since 1951. There are ten other states where these responsibilities are assumed by the legislative council. In addition the legislative council in Arkansas is responsible for preparing the budget, and a Texas Legislative Budget Board prepares a budget as an alternative to the executive budget. There are several states (Indiana, Idaho, Mississippi, and South Carolina) in which members of the legislature serve on the commission that prepares the budget.[13] In several states, including New York and Florida, legislators attend the formal hearings of the budget agency or commission at which agencies make their requests for funds; members of the legislative budget staff attend such hearings in a number of states. New York uses nine joint fiscal subcommittees for year-round supervision of agencies and their spending.

It is difficult to generalize about budgetary practices that vary so much from state to state and that have not been the subject of extensive research. In a number of the

states the staff employed by legislative budget committees is too small (at least by comparison with those
employed by the executive budget agency) for a comprehensive study. Seldom do the appropriations committees
devote enough time and study to become thoroughly familiar with state budgets. But, as the legislatures become
more professional and better staffed, these deficiencies
can be overcome. The Joint Legislative Budget Committee in California provides an example of the scope and
quality of budgetary review that is possible in the legislature. The committee appoints a legislative analyst, who
heads a staff of thirty specialists with a half-million dollar
budget. He supervises a detailed analysis of the budget as
well as research projects pertinent to the budgetary process. The members of his office also serve as a staff for the
Senate and House committees that act on the budget. It is
the legislative analyst's responsibility to inform the Joint
Committee of administrative failures to fulfill the intent of
previous legislation and to call attention to appropriations
requests that have previously been denied by the legislature or that constitute new services. Probably his most
important responsibility is to make detailed recommendations concerning the executive budget; he may recom-
mend approval or disapproval, increase or decrease, in
each proposed item of expenditure, or he may suggest
that more information should be required to substantiate
the request. The legislative analyst receives all the data
from individual agencies that are supplied to the budget
office, and members of his staff attend all the budget
hearings.[14]

The Texas Legislative Budget Board differs because it
actually prepares a budget and an appropriations bill,

while the California legislative analyst only makes specific recommendations on the executive budget. But in both states we have examples of agents, selected by the legislature, that offer the legislature a detailed and carefully prepared alternative to the governor's budget. In both cases it may be more important for individual agencies to present a persuasive case to the legislative agency than to the executive budgetary authority.

We should distinguish between two principal purposes of legislative review of proposed expenditures. The first purpose is to review the levels of efficiency and economy in an agency and determine whether previous and proposed expenditures are in accord with legislative intentions. The legislature wants to know whether sound principles of competitive bidding are being followed, whether administrators are too extravagant in providing travel allowances for their subordinates, whether funds are being diverted to projects not visualized by the legislature, and whether increases in appropriations will increase the opportunities for wasting or misdirecting funds. Such supervision is possible if the legislative staff work is adequate and if the legislative committees reward virtue and punish waste when they make appropriations. In addition over half of the states require a post-audit of expenditures by an agency that is responsible to the legislature.

A second and more fundamental objective of legislative review is to exercise independent judgment about the distribution of state funds and, as an inevitable consequence, about the priority that should be accorded to various state programs. Better staffing can clarify the choices that have to be made, but the responsibility for making the choice—or simply accepting the governor's recommendation—lies with the legislature. One frustration that faces legislative budget committees (as well as executive budget agencies) is the large proportion of state revenues—exceeding one-half in some states—that is earmarked for specific purposes. The legislature has the power, but probably not the inclination, to remove most of these obstacles to budgetary supervision. In the past, as we have noted, state expenditures have been largely devoted to certain traditional purposes, such as highways, education, and welfare. Most of these programs have grown so steadily, with population growth and higher standards of state service, that there has been little opportunity for new and original programs of governmental spending. Most of the new programs that have been inaugurated by the states have been in response to federal grant-in-aid programs. In short, neither the executive nor the legislature has had much flexibility, and there have been relatively few occasions for significant debates between the two branches of government over the scope and direction of state spending. The legislative appropriations committees have been reluctant to cut back, or prevent normal expansion of, the traditional state programs; at the same time these committees have not been advocates of new programs.

The growing demands for state programs to serve metropolitan needs, demands that are being heard more clearly in the legislature, may lead to a more active legislative role in the budgetary process. Interest groups that have been rebuffed by those who make executive budgets may turn for help to their allies in the legislature, as comparable groups do in Congress. It is possible that legislative appropriations committees, as a consequence, will become more concerned with the substantive questions of budgeting and not merely with the need for efficiency and economy.

Will the growth of effective budgetary review by adequately staffed legislative committees undermine the executive budget? Will the governor's ability to use the budget as a centralizing tool of administration be destroyed because the agencies can appeal his decisions to a legislative committee whose recommendation will be accepted by the legislature? We should recognize that several different factors may explain the legislature's adoption of a well-staffed budget review committee. One may be a belief that the legislature must fill a gap created by the failure of the governor to create and adequately staff a strong budget agency. On the other hand, the legislature may decide that the governor has been so successful in centralizing the budget function, and providing it with staff, that the legislature must establish and staff a committee that is loyal and responsible to it, and that can provide expert advice on the budget. In some cases the legislature's refusal to follow the governor's lead may be motivated by political differences.[15]

One authority has concluded: "in states where the governor has ignored the budget function and left the initiative to the legislature [and] . . . where the legislative staff is competent, it is difficult for the governor to build his own budget staff and to regain his lost prerogative." In states where the governor has not exercised firm budgetary control, there would be greater likelihood that agencies would shift their attention to the legislative budgetary committees. "On the other hand, in states where strong budget offices have been established first, it is unlikely that legislative budget analysts will gain primacy in the budgetary process." [16]

The impact of legislative review on the governor's budgetary authority will also be affected by political factors. In Texas, for example, one former governor concluded that under the dual budget system adopted in that state "the governor's submission of a budget is little more than a formality, and, by and large, budgeting is done by the legislators." Governor John B. Connally, however, whose position in the legislature was strong and whose budget director had come from the legislative budget staff, was able to gain adoption of most of his appropriations requests in 1965.[17] The establishment of a more elaborate and better staffed structure for legislative review in New York is a direct result of accumulated legislative distrust of the governor, resulting from the conflicts between Governor Averell Harriman and the Republican legislature and the subsequent clashes over taxes between Governor Nelson Rockefeller and the legislature.

As long as the governor is able to maintain political strength in the legislature as well as in the executive branch, the legislature will be unlikely to make sweeping changes in his budgetary proposals, no matter how conscientiously the legislative committees do their job. The item veto, available to the governor in thirty-eight states, helps to maintain his control over executive agencies by restricting their ability to get larger funds from the legislative branch. The weak governor, or one who is engaged in a political battle with the legislature, is likely to discover that the legislature is increasingly able to effect changes in his budget. Even the governor who is politically strong will encounter more conflict in the legislature over his budget because the pressures for higher state spending, particularly in the metropolitan areas, will intensify.

Responsible Legislative Power

Obviously the legislature that is better organized and staffed and that meets for longer periods of time will have a variety of opportunities for encroaching on the governor's prerogatives or harassing executive agencies. It may pass legislation that is so detailed as to hamstring the rule-making authority and curtail the administrative flexibility of executive agencies. It may conduct detailed committee investigations into administrative decision-making, ranging from political favoritism in the personnel policies of the highway department to university regulations concerning political speeches on the campus. It is also possible that alliances between individual legislators or legislative committees and executive agencies will be strengthened and will undermine the governor's executive authority and his ability to win legislative support for his programs. There is no certainty that the higher pay scales and other incentives will attract more qualified men to the legislature, and if this does not happen, many supporters of legislative reform may become dubious about giving the legislature broader scope in which to operate and more months in which to occupy the capitol.

The American Assembly said that its "focus on the state legislature by no means implies a derogation of the executive. Strengthening each branch strengthens all by contributing to a strong state government." [18] We may question whether this is literally true, but we should also recognize that the legislature does not need to be strengthened at the expense of the governor. A good argument can be made that if either branch of government is strengthened care should be taken to maintain some balance of power with the other branch—that the goal of the reformer should be a strong legislature *and* a strong governor.

We need to be concerned not merely with the distribution of power but with its responsible use. The best argument for a strong governor is that he is more visible and can more readily be held accountable to the voters than can a flock of elected officials and independent boards. The best protection against the abuse of power by a strong governor is a legislature that is not only competent but is organized along partisan lines. The opposition party guarantees that the governor's proposals will be scrutinized and sometimes criticized; the administration party guarantees that they will not be ignored. Moreover, a partisan legislature is more visible and more accountable to the voter. The legislative process is usually too complex for the voter to understand, and the record of individual legislators is too obscure for even the interested citizen to discover. But it is possible for the voter to become aware of the major accomplishments or failures of the party majority in the legislature and to cast an intelligent vote on the basis of this knowledge. In that sense partisanship makes the legislature responsible to the voters.

It is true that we know very little about legislative responsibility: how the voters perceive candidates and how they make choices in state elections, how they communicate to legislatures, and what they know about the record of the legislature. We are only beginning to explore the legislative system in all its complexity and subtlety. There are few studies devoted to the nature of partisanship in the legislature, and most of these go no further than measuring roll calls. As legislatures begin to fit the two-party pattern and as the constituent bases and sources of cohesion in many legislative parties undergo change, the time is certainly ripe for more thorough scholarly exploration of the legislative party.

The legislature of today and tomorrow will be more responsive than that of the past in another respect: it will be more responsive to the needs of metropolitan areas. However difficult it may be to measure the impact of malapportionment in years past, it cannot be doubted that malapportioned legislatures left most of the problems of the metropolis to be solved—or simply ignored—by other levels of government. These problems are so serious, and the access of metropolitan interests to the legislature has now been so increased, that the legislature cannot escape them—whatever decisions it makes about their solution. It is no accident that the demand for more competent legislators has become so strong at the present moment, or that this demand has been most insistent in the larger states. There is a need for better trained, more experienced, and better staffed legislators who will devote more time to their job, primarily because the problems created by the metropolitan society are so vast and so pressing—and so clearly the business of the state legislature—that they demand a new level of legislative excellence.

IV

The Decline of States' Rights
and the
Rise of State Administration

Daniel R. Grant

WE ARE LIVING IN THE MIDST OF WHAT IS, on the surface at least, a very puzzling American paradox in national–state relations. It is the paradox of states' decline and states' growth, of dramatic, repeated, and overwhelming defeats of assertions of states' rights and of equally dramatic growth of state government. If one were seeking a Madison Avenue title for an analysis of the decline of states' rights and the rise of state administration he would perhaps be tempted to call it "Up the Down Staircase." In any case, it is appropriate to begin with a discussion of the "downward" and "upward" elements of the paradox.

The Succession of Losing Battles with the National Government over States' Rights

It is certainly no secret that in American history the overwhelming majority of issues involving states' rights have been ultimately decided against the states. Major battles have been lost not only in military conflagrations from Appomattox to Little Rock, Oxford, and Tuscaloosa, but also in the courts, the Congress, and the White House. It is difficult to point to any surviving major constitutional protection for the doctrine of states' rights. One such protection was the original distinction between interstate commerce (the area of national regulatory authority) and intrastate commerce (the area of state regulatory authority). The erosion of this distinction began early in the nineteenth century, and the twentieth century growth of a national economy has doubtless convinced the Supreme Court that little meaningful distinction remains.

Another strong constitutional protection for states' rights was the concept of delegated powers for the national government and reserved powers for the states or the people. Chief Justice John Marshall got us off to an early start in broadening the concept of delegated powers by enunciating the doctrine of implied powers in the so-called "elastic" or "necessary and proper" clause—and the elastic has been stretching ever since. Although the principal power reserved to the states is the police power—the power to provide for the health, welfare, safety, morals, and convenience of the people—we find increasing reference in textbooks to the national government's "quasi-police power." This is a reference to a kind of *de facto* police power that has grown up through use of the national taxing power, spending power, commerce power, war power, postal power, and even treaty power (*Missouri* v. *Holland* [1]) for the purposes of regulating, prohibiting, or attacking such diverse evils as gambling, kidnapping, urban blight, stealing automobiles, killing migratory birds, poverty, firing an employee because of labor union membership or activities, and refusing public accommodations to a person because of his race. Indeed, it is difficult to think of any area included in the traditional state police power that could not be the subject of national legislation under one of its presently recognized powers.

The summary of losing battles would not be complete without at least passing reference to some windmill jousting on behalf of what were obviously lost causes before they began, at least in the minds of most historians. I am referring to three *alleged* constitutional protections for states' rights—the "doctrines" of nullification, secession, and interposition. Each doctrine was sufficiently appealing to attract strong emotional support and to constitute a tremendous political weapon, and each eventually went down to unconditional and total defeat. Defiance of court orders and "standing in the doorway" in the name of interposition may have delayed school desegregation a bit, and may have saved political face more than a bit, but it demonstrated both to believers and to nonbelievers the doctrine of states' rights at its worst, constitutionally and morally. The states, as states, suffered not only a constitutional defeat but a propaganda defeat.

Two of the most recent defeats administered to the advocates of states' rights came in the form of the Civil Rights Act of 1964 and the Voting Rights Act of 1965. The latter authorized extensive intervention by federal voting registrars to prevent the use of literacy tests to bar Negroes from registering to vote. The 1964 Act was aimed at ending discrimination in employment practices and in public accommodations, and authorized the cutting off of federal funds to state and local governments that continue to discriminate in their programs. When the Supreme

Court upheld the use of the commerce power to forbid racial discrimination in places of public accommodation (*Heart of Atlanta Motel, Inc.* v. *United States* [2]), columnist David Lawrence charged that "what many historians will describe as a Federal dictatorship was set up in the United States" [3] on December 14, 1964. The *Washington Post*, on the other hand, stated that the Court had rendered "a great national service," [4] and the *New York Times* described the opinion as "a profoundly important victory for the cause of justice in our society." [5]

Funeral Orations and Last Rites Said for the States

Just as David Lawrence seemed to interpret the passing and upholding of the Civil Rights Act of 1964 as the beginning of a federal dictatorship, in a similar manner others have interpreted the earlier defeats for the states' rights position as the death knell for states and the end of any meaningful federalism. Sometimes the last rites have been pronounced by friends of states' rights; on other occasions it has been friends of national power who have said "the states are dying, if not already dead."

As early as 1886 John W. Burgess wrote that the states were declining because they were not one of the two natural elements in our system—the community and the nation.[6] Charles E. Merriam had strong doubts about the future of states, and in 1928 wrote "the state . . . is standing upon very slippery ground as a political unit. . . . The nation and the city," he added, "are vigorous organs, but the state is not." [7] Still another political scientist went out on a limb in 1933 to declare: "it is a matter of brutal record. The American state is finished. I do not predict that the states will go, but affirm that they have gone." [8] In 1941

George C. S. Benson wrote that the states are the core of American federalism, but expressed fear the the core "is rotting." [9] The late Leonard D. White was never considered an alarmist, at least not until 1953 when he wrote: "if present trends continue for another quarter century, the states may be left hollow shells, operating primarily as field districts of federal departments and dependent upon the federal treasury for their support." [10]

Even stronger funeral orations have come from staunch advocates of states' rights, such as James J. Kilpatrick, who wrote in 1957 that if the states do not regain the powers of "State sovereignty that died at Appomattox," the alternative is "for American government to grow steadily more centralized, steadily more remote from the people, steadily more monolithic and despotic." [11] In opposing the passage of federal aid to education in 1961, Senator A. Willis Robertson of Virginia predicted: "individual and States' rights—already wavering under Federal onslaught—will be further imperiled when education itself becomes the tool of a central authority." [12] In opposing a constitutional amendment to abolish the state poll tax as a voting requirement, Senator Richard Russell of Georgia expressed resentment of efforts to "take away and circumscribe the few rights that the States have left," and expressed fear that we will "destroy the Federal system by making the States impotent and constituting mere geographical areas that are designated from Washington. . . ." [13]

Perhaps it is appropriate to conclude these pessimistic appraisals of the status of the states with a statement that might sound familiar to a southern audience: "There is scarce[ly] a domain in the field of government properly belonging to the municipality or the state, which the federal government is not seeking to invade by the use of the specious phrase 'federal aid.' . . . This rapid extension of federal administration not only means greatly increased expense because of duplication of efforts, but it means the gradual breaking down of local self-government in America." [14] Those who suspect that this quotation came from an incumbent southern governor are wrong, for it was actually a statement by the governor of Illinois during the presidential term of one who was hardly a notorious New Deal radical, Warren G. Harding. The governor was Frank Lowden, writing in 1921.

Dramatic Growth of State Government

These funeral orations and last rites have the strange ring of unreality about them when placed in the context of the hard data on state and local growth during the past fifteen to twenty years. In striking contrast to the "states-are-dead theory" are these opening lines of a recent article on intergovernmental relations:

> The largest growth sector in the United States during the past decade has been:
> Defense? No.
> Space? No.
> Automobile manufacturing? Not even warm.
> Federal government? Wrong again.
> State and local government? Right. [15]

This may seem strange indeed, but the rate of growth of state and local governments, since the end of World War II, has been greater than that of the national government. Just since 1950 state expenditures have more than tripled, jumping from $15.5 billion to $51 billion, when aid to local governments is included. City and other local governments have expanded at a similar pace. State and

local expenditures between 1902 and 1966 rose phenome-
nally from $1.0 billion to almost $95 billion. Although
the national government has spent more annually than
state and local governments since about 1935, the recent
upsurge in state and local spending has narrowed the gap
considerably. The ratio now stands at about fifty-eight to
forty-two for the $225 billion total for all levels of govern-
ment. In the case of revenues collected, the gap between
the two is wider, but even here the share collected by
state and local governments has been steadily increasing.
These surprising facts of fiscal life have not gone unno-
ticed by nationally organized taxpayers whose watchdog
activities have been focused mainly on the national government. A committee of the National Association of
Manufacturers, reporting on the 1967 federal budget,
cited the much greater acceleration of purchases of goods
and services by state and local governments in the past
decade ($36.6 billion to $68.2 billion) than by the national government ($45.6 billion to $66.7 billion).[16]

In number of employees the comparison is also striking.
While federal employment of civilians (nearly 2.9 million
in 1966) has risen only slightly since 1950, state and local
governmental employment has doubled (4.3 million
to 8.6 million) in the same period. Even if the 4.4
million public education employees should be subtracted,
state and local governments employ far more persons than
does the federal government.

The paradoxical picture is thus complete. Despite "centralization" and "the eclipse of states' rights," state governments are spending more money, employing more
people, doing more things of greater impact, and are apparently more important now than ever before in American history. In short, we must conclude that the states, if
by some miraculous means they were given the powers of

speech, would say in much the same manner as Mark Twain: "reports of my death are greatly exaggerated." More than this, we must recognize that states have actually grown rather than declined.

It is important to pause at this point, in the midst of painting the picture of this striking paradox, and warn against overstating or oversimplifying it. There is a sense in which the states have declined in a *relative* weighing of national and state leadership and initiative in public policy formulation as well as of national and state constitutional authority. The future growth and prestige of the states is still by no means assured, but it is clear that we can discard the modern mythology about the death or insignificance of the states, insofar as the present or near future is concerned. And it becomes increasingly important to recognize the strong growth of public administration in state government.

If the result of the many federal victories at the expense of states has not been the death or even diminution of state administration, what, then, has been the effect? There are obviously many ways to examine the effects. The discussion which follows will focus briefly on two related things: (1) the effect of older federal aid programs on state administration, and (2) recent developments and friction points in federal–state relations.

THE IMPACT OF FEDERAL AID ON STATE ADMINISTRATION

Effects of the Older Programs

In considering the effects of federal-aid programs on state administration, it is useful to examine first the effects up to an approximate mid-point in the twentieth century.

Federal aid programs by this time seemed to have settled into fairly well accepted patterns; moreover the year 1953 was the occasion for the first really comprehensive study of federal-aid programs and federal–state relations. This study, by the United States Commission on Intergovernmental Relations (known popularly as the Kestnbaum Commission), was concerned with many more things than just the impact of federal aid on state administration, but it does provide some important clues on this subject at mid-century.

Before we consider its findings, we should remember that the Kestnbaum Commission was not created for the purpose of defending federal aid either in theory or in practice; nor was it created with any expectation that it would justify centralization of governmental powers from lower to higher levels. Actually, there was good reason to expect just the opposite result, when one considers the political context of its creation and particularly the appointment of Clarence Manion as its first chairman. There was ample reason to expect the study to reflect a strong states' rights orientation and to put great emphasis on returning national programs and powers to state and local government. Manion's resignation (under pressure), and his replacement with Meyer Kestnbaum as chairman, was probably more effect than cause, but it symbolizes a more moderate, middle-of-the-road outlook of the Commission on federal–state relations. Even so, it seems clear that the Kestnbaum Commission had no pro-centralization bias and made every effort to uncover all possible evidence of dissatisfaction with existing federal aid programs.

Several of the findings growing out of the Kestnbaum studies point to direct or indirect effects of the older aid programs on state administration. First of all, they discovered and emphasized that there is great diversity in the impact of federal aid, both from state to state and from program to program. In retrospect, diversity should not have been surprising when one considers the enormous differences among the states in wealth, urbanization, administrative professionalization and maturity, and political party systems. But opponents of federal aid, in simplifying their philosophical arguments, had tended to paint a picture of a monolithic, homogenized leviathan whose end product was all states in a single mold. The discovery of such diversity of federal-aid impact became a two-fold problem—a research problem for the staff of the Commission, and a political problem for opponents of federal aid, who had been painting more simple pictures. The Kestnbaum Commission's report even gives a rather sympathetic treatment of their finding that at first glance "existing Federal grant programs look like a hodge-podge," by adding that the grants do not constitute a system, "and indeed ... they were never intended to make up a system." [17] The report stressed that federal grants-in-aid have been used primarily to accomplish specific and varied national objectives, and not merely to help states and local governments finance their activities.

A second category of findings of the Kestnbaum Commission concerns the impact of federal aid on state personnel and personnel administration. One of the staff studies, for example, concluded: "there seems to be little question that Federal aid has stimulated professionalism in the State agencies concerned." [18] The specific requirements concerning personnel in federally aided programs had two major effects: (1) to encourage political neutrality, and (2) to require "the technical dimensions of the merit system." [19] Concerning the former, it would be unrealistic to suggest overwhelming success of the extension of Hatch Act prohibitions on political activities to state employees paid from federal funds, but it would be safe to speak of this objective as partially accomplished. The requirement that state employees be recruited and retained according to merit principles has not been extended to all federally aided programs—it began with the Social Security Act in 1939—but a recent estimate gives the requirement credit for stimulating the creation of merit systems for "perhaps as many as three-quarters of a million public employees in State and local governments." [20] In general, however, the merit requirements have not been applied to as many employees as has the requirement for political neutrality.

The Kestnbaum Commission sought to assess the impact of these federal personnel requirements on state administration in general—that is, to the nonfederally aided departments of the states. The conclusion from their efforts was that "there is no clear answer," but the following mixed items of evidence are illustrative of their difficulty in arriving at any consensus on such questions:

> In West Virginia and many other states, such practices have not spread to nonaided agencies. . . . In imitation of the merit system in federally aided agencies in Iowa, a similar merit system with some modifications has been established for the other agencies. [In Kentucky] . . . the introduction of merit principles may have influenced the spread of the merit system to a few agencies that do not receive Federal aid.
>
> In States which have a general merit system, differentials in salaries and other conditions of employment are less between grant and non-grant receiving

agencies than is true of States which do not have a general merit system. The dual personnel system is a source of some antagonism in Texas and in various other States where the merit principle is far from statewide acceptance. It was generally admitted that the aided services tend to develop professionalism but there was wide difference of views on the "Federal loyalties" question. ... [In] Kentucky and South Dakota ... [It was contended] that personnel in grant–administering agencies tended to develop "Federal loyalties" to the detriment of overall State interests; and there were minority opinions to the same effect in Idaho and elsewhere. But on the whole it was felt that professionalism is not carried so far as to develop a "Federal loyalty" at the expense of overall State interests. Where such loyalty is alleged to exist, it is usually the State employment security agency which is pointed to, an agency whose administrative costs are wholly financed by Federal grants.[21]

A third area of potential impact studied by the Kestnbaum Commission was state administrative organization. Two of the commission's survey reports dealt with this question and concluded that, with several exceptions, "overall State administrative reorganization has neither been helped nor hindered by Federal aid but that reorganization of a particular function has been helped by the Federal 'single agency' requirement."[22] The Governors' Conference, in its 1961 annual meeting, indicated disagreement with this conclusion, and approved a resolution deploring "the tendency of Federal agencies to dictate the organizational form and structure through which the

States carry out federally supported programs." [23] It requested an investigation by the Council of State Governments of federal requirements dealing with state organization. The Council reported in 1962 that federal grants have had a minor influence on state governmental structure and organization. It added, however, that this influence has on occasion been an obstacle to state administrative reorganization for the purpose of co-ordinating state functions. [24] One of the Kestnbaum reports had cited incidents in which state opponents of administrative reorganization had used federal requirements as an argument for the status quo, but it was suggested that much of this was merely campaign oratory rather than actual federal requirements.

The common requirement that states designate a single agency to administer or supervise a given program was said by the Kestnbaum Commission to have proved generally satisfactory. It was critical, however, of two instances in which grant-in-aid statutes require states to administer programs through state commissions. Nevertheless, the overall conclusion is to deny adverse effects of federal grants on the unity of the state executive process, and they contended this was true both for strong–governor and weak–governor situations.

Federal aid was not given such a clean bill of health in its impact on state fiscal management. It was reported that federal grants, while not preventing the introduction and use of an executive budget system, do complicate the budget with a multiplicity of separate federal appropriation items, different state and federal fiscal years, uncertainties about Congressional appropriations, and requirements that states earmark revenues from specified sources to support the federal programs. The Kestnbaum Commis-

sion took note also of the charge by a number of state
budget officers that grants-in-aid distort state budgets,
but concluded from its own studies: "neither the nature
nor the extent of the distortion . . . is entirely clear." [25]

Several other effects of federal aid were cited by the
Kestnbaum Commission, some of them only indirectly
related to administration at the state level. The assignment
in one study was to discover whether federal aid had
tended to diminish the political importance of governors
and the conclusion was that the governor's political role
"seems to have been enhanced by Federal aid because it
enables the State to provide more and better services. This
tends to increase the stature and influence of the Governor
in the eyes of the citizens." [26] On the question of effect
on the involvement of citizens, parties, and interest groups,
it was said that federally aided programs had apparently
led to some increased interest and participation in government. On the very basic "sixty-four dollar question" of
whether federal aid had actually contributed significantly
to centralization of government, the Commission seemed
to deny that grants had been essentially a centralizing
mechanism for encroachment on states' rights. The Commission recognized that there is "a risk that State participation in joint schemes, while bolstering the States as
going organizations, may induce habits of subordination
and deference to external initiative and guidance." [27] They
concluded: "in the long run this risk is less serious for the
States than the effects of being bypassed," and suggested
that centralization is more a product of other factors than
it is a result of federal aid. From this viewpoint, federal
grants-in-aid to the states might even be considered devices to avoid greater centralization. [28]

By way of summary, it can be said that state administration during the first half of the twentieth century was generally larger, broader in its scope of activities, and more professional in its outlook as a result of the growth of federal aid programs. By the same token neither the extravagant hopes for panacea nor the fearful charges of tyranny were borne out by the facts of actual experience. On the whole the report of the Kestnbaum Commission seemed to be a surprisingly strong defense of the status quo as federal grants-in-aid had developed and, for the most part, a refutation of the more serious arguments against them. The Commission had come a long way from the direction toward which the first chairman, Clarence Manion, seemed to have been pointing it.

Recent Developments in Federal–State Relations

Thus far our focus has been primarily on federal–state relations as of about 1955. It is in order now to consider where we are in the mid-1960's, and to see whether or not there is a need to rewrite or add contemporary footnotes to the "Kestnbaum script." In general the picture of the past decade is one of tremendous growth, experimentation, change, and proliferation of federal aid programs. The growth reached virtual tidal wave proportions after 1960, bringing the total number of separate programs to more than 170, administered by twenty-one federal departments and agencies. Between 1957 and 1967 the outlay increased from $4 billion to $14.5 billion. This proliferation of new programs has quite literally required the proverbial "score card to identify the players" and has made a "best seller" out of the Government Printing Office's *Catalog of Federal Aids to State and Local Governments,* published in 1964 and supplemented annually since.

More specifically, what are the more distinctive characteristics of recent federal–state relations? Several had become clear by the end of 1966:

1. *Greater Urban Orientation Than Ever Before.* The trend toward stronger urban emphasis has, of course, been growing for many years in such federal aid programs as highways, housing, urban renewal, airports, and pollution control, but 1965 was a high water mark in new federal legislation with urban implications. Not only was a new cabinet Department of Housing and Urban Development created, but the same measure granted authority for basic water and sewer facilities, advance acquisition of land, open space preservation, urban beautification, codes enforcement assistance, rent supplements, demolition of unsafe structures, and support for councils of elected local officials. In 1966 the still broader urban program embodying the concept of demonstration cities was authorized (with the term "model cities" being preferred more recently to avoid the possible invidious connotation of "demonstrations").

2. *Larger Federal Financial Participation.* An increasing number of programs now go beyond the traditional fifty-fifty federal sharing arrangement with the states. The interstate highway program provides for a federal share of 90 percent; the first three titles of the elementary and secondary education aid program requires no matching at all; the Economic Opportunity Act authorizes 90 percent as the federal share in work-training and work-study programs; and other examples could be given of the increasing size of the federal share in aid programs.

3. *Increased Emphasis on Relating Grant Programs to Comprehensive Planning and Co-ordination.* These are two separate but related characteristics of the newer aid

programs. The requirement or encouragement of *comprehensive* planning (not merely planning) in connection with federal aid programs is more common than specific requirements to co-ordinate with other programs and units of government, but both are aimed at meeting the criticism of excessive "*ad hoc* autonomy" for federal aid projects. The Clean Water Program and the Economic Development Program, both authorized in 1965, offer an incentive of an additional 10 percent grant for projects certified as being in conformity with a comprehensive plan. An example of federal support for inter-agency co-ordination is the "preference provision" of the Economic Opportunity Act of 1965, which specifies that preference in all federal grants shall be given to projects that are parts of an approved "community action" program.

4. *Use of the Multi-functional Approach.* A modest approach to co-ordination at the federal level of at least some of the aid programs is found in the creation of two new agencies. The Department of Housing and Urban Development is charged with co-ordinating not only its own programs but also other federal activities that bear on urban development. Similarly, the Office of Economic Opportunity (OEO) is legally responsible for co-ordinating the anti-poverty programs of other agencies as well as those administered by the OEO itself. Simply to specify co-ordination in the law in this manner by no means guarantees that it will take place, but it has undoubtedly caused greater awareness of, and concern for, the problem of co-ordinating many related programs.

5. *New "Move-or-Else" Warnings to the States.* After years of painfully slow progress in such areas as stream pollution control, new federal aid programs have been enacted with "we-will-act-if-you-don't" provisions. The Water Quality Act of 1965 gave the states two years to

adopt acceptable water quality criteria and plans for implementation, with the clear alternative of federal action if such state action were not taken. Highway safety legislation passed in 1966 gave the states until the end of 1968 to adopt an approved safety program, but the penalty is loss of 10 percent of the state's federal aid highway funds rather than the establishment of a federal safety program. A similar penalty provision was included in the Highway Beautification Act of 1965, aimed at securing state action banning billboards and screening or removing junkyards along interstate and primary highways.

6. *Federal Entry into New Fields.* Recent federal–state relations are characterized not only by new methods and emphases in the older program areas, but by major federal entry into programs with little or no previous federal involvement. Congress finally pierced the "sound barrier" of direct and general aid to education at the elementary and secondary level when in 1965 it authorized the first *general* aid to education ever enacted. Also precedent-breaking was the Higher Education Facilities Act of 1963, which may prove to be as much a turning point for American colleges and universities as was the passage of the Morrill [land-grant college] Act a century earlier. Federal aid for education prior to 1963 had been approached gingerly *through* higher education for ancillary purposes such as research, educating veterans, training scientists, or training foreign language teachers. The 1963 Act took a long step in the direction of aid *for* higher education by authorizing grants directly for faculty development, facilities, and student aid other than loans.

The War on Poverty had an especially high birth rate of new programs in its first two or three years, and their "newness" is a reflection of the basic goal of dealing with causes rather than symptoms of poverty. As a result, many of its accomplishments and its problems may be traced to this emphasis on creativity and a break with the past. Another innovation is found in the attention given to regional aspects of poverty by the Area Redevelopment Act of 1961 and, more specifically, the Appalachian Regional Development Act of 1965. The Appalachian program is an interesting departure from past practice not only in its being focused on a single hard–core poverty region, involving twelve states, but in its being based on a new concept of co-operative federalism. Major decisions in initiating, supervising, and co-ordinating various economic redevelopment projects are delegated to the participating states in the Appalachian Regional Commission, with an unusual arrangement for decisions by a majority of the states, subject to a veto by a federal representative designated by the President.

Other new fields entered by the federal government in recent years include highway beautification, air pollution control, water pollution control, open space preservation, and new areas of correctional administration.

7. *Other Distinctive Characteristics of Recent Federal–State Relations.* Among the more important characteristics of recent federal aid programs are increased involvement of *private* agencies and institutions, the recurrence of direct federal–local relations tending to by-pass the states, and stronger involvement in racial issues. These topics are discussed in more detail below.

Current Friction Points in Federal–State Administrative Relations

It is much too early to appraise the impact of these new programs on state administration, but it is not too early to identify the major points of friction—or "squeak points," as they are sometimes called. The following seem to be the major ones:

1. *Stronger Involvement in Racial Issues.* Public administrators at the state and local levels have been caught in a crossfire between federal administrative requirements and state and local political pressures with respect to racial problems. The capacity of administrators to reconcile the interests and demands of organized "white power" and "black power" groups in such programs as education, urban renewal, and the war on poverty has become increasingly restricted. Tension over federal guidelines concerning racial aspects of these programs can be expected to persist and perhaps even increase so long as this hot potato continues to be passed between the executive, legislative, and judicial branches of government.

2. *Increase in Direct Federal–Local Relations, By-passing the States.* City government representatives have long criticized state involvement in federal aid programs as a useless fifth wheel at best and as an obstructionist element at worst. In previous years the tendency to by-pass the states was strongest in the case of urban-oriented programs such as airport assistance, and it is the strong urban emphasis in the more recent tidal wave of legislation which has raised the issue again. This time the states have had an articulate "outside" spokesman against their being by-passed—the United States Advisory Commission on Intergovernmental Relations. The reports of this agency have generally opposed any move to by-pass the states or downgrade their role in the new "creative federalism." The Commission's advice to the states, however, has been refreshingly realistic in that it has argued that

the states must "buy" their way into these programs both by means of financial participation and by the provision of meaningful technical assistance. While it may once have been unreasonable to expect these conditions to be met, the prospects are considerably enhanced by the recent increased urban representation in state legislatures.

3. *Increase in Direct Federal–Private Relations.* The increasing number and variety of federal grants going directly to private agencies and institutions, including religious ones, have added to the complications of administrative and political co-ordination and democratic control. With the majority of urban community anti-poverty problems being co-ordinated by nonpublic or quasi-public "umbrella agencies," it seems clear that a Pandora's box is being created with respect to the already complex problem of metropolitan intergovernmental relations, not to mention the usual complexities of vertical relations in the federal system. Added to these are the traditional tensions over whether specific programs constitute a violation of the constitutional principle of separation of church and state. A kind of "private federalism" thus seems to be developing alongside the more traditional public federalism.

4. *The Governor's Veto Power over Anti-Poverty Projects.* A running controversy has developed over whether to permit governors to veto particular anti-poverty projects. After a brief experience with permissive legislation to this effect, a compromise change limited the scope of the veto and made it subject to over-riding by the OEO director. Hardly a happy arrangement for those committed to the idea of state sovereignty and to the prerogatives of state governors, the situation seems likely to be a continuing point of tension.

5. *Increased Competition Between All Levels of Government for Tax Sources.* There is nothing really new about competition between levels of government for revenue sources, but the growth of state and local services, expenditures, payrolls, and debts has acutely aggravated this friction point. Increased discussion can be expected of various schemes for federal tax sharing with state and local governments with few strings or no strings involved, such as the "Heller Plan," "Laird Plan," and others. The proposals vary greatly in degree of coercion and equalization proposed, but all seek to alleviate the problem of intergovernmental tax competition.

6. *"Grantsmanship" and the State and Local Manpower Crisis.* Increasingly the only way for state and local governments to stay on top of the growing complexity of federal aid programs, with their infinite variety of program requirements, is to have an extensive pool of well-trained public servants who are adept at applying for federal grants. The game of "grantsmanship" with all of its intricate stratagems has been criticized as tending to favor the wealthier, better staffed states and cities to the disadvantage of other areas where the need tends to be the greatest. In a relative sense, at least, the rich seem to get richer and the poor poorer. Others criticize the "project-itis" tendencies of federal aid programs, charging that continuity and co-ordination are difficult to attain because of this *ad hoc* emphasis of federal aid.

7. *Vertical Lines Complicating Horizontal Co-ordination.* The charge is sometimes made that growing federal–state–local vertical ties within given subject-matter areas are making it increasingly difficult to achieve administrative co-ordination in the office of governor, mayor, or city manager. It is said that professionalization segments ad-

ministration badly enough without having the further complication of increasingly strong federal–state–local administrative relationships.

8. *The Absence of a Consistent Philosophy of the Role of the State in Federal Aid Programs.* Norman Beckman recently took an inventory of the various state roles in different federal aid programs. The following catalogue of diverse state roles is the result: a "channel" in "701" * planning assistance to smaller communities; a "priority–setter" in sewage treatment and hospital construction grants; a "planner" in the federal aid highway program; a "partner" in the River Basin Commission title of the Water Resources Planning Act; an "approving body" in the Land and Water Conservation Fund; a "legislative enabler" for most of the programs of the Department of Housing and Urban Development; and a "nonparticipant" in the Farmers Home Administration's grant and loan program for waterworks and sewage disposal plants.[29] Then Beckman turns pragmatist and contends that the system is working reasonably well in spite of all the tension points. He suggests a paraphrasing of Emerson: "A foolish consistency in Federal–State relations will continue to be the hobgoblin of little minds, adored by little statesmen and philosophers." [30]

Prospects for Easing the Tensions

There are on the horizon some rays of hope at the state level for those interested in easing federal–state tensions. Some are not sufficiently developed to merit being called "trends," but others give every evidence of being impor-

---

* "701" grants refer to urban planning assistance authorized originally in the Federal Housing Act of 1954, Section 701.

tant forces in the political and administrative future of federalism. The creation and early direction of the Advisory Commission on Intergovernmental Relations (ACIR) seems in itself to be a good omen for the states. It has had a much stronger urban interest than the Kestnbaum Commission and the ill-fated Joint Federal–State Action Committee, but it has maintained a strong commitment to the importance of state governments as such. The choice of Frank Bane as chairman of ACIR had the effect of placing "Mister State Government" in a key role during its formative years. As a permanent agency with a broad intergovernmental political base, the ACIR should provide the lubricant for many of the squeak points in the federal system.

Another encouraging development is the creation of state offices of local affairs and state offices of co-ordination for federal aid programs. States are increasingly turning to this administrative mechanism because of the involvement of several departments in a single federal aid program. The anti-poverty program is the chief instigator for such state co-ordination efforts, with a governor's aide in several states being delegated the liaison job. States are beginning to create offices of local affairs, though it is ironic that the movement has lagged behind the national government's creation of the cabinet-level Department of Housing and Urban Development. A related development, but one that is far from being in full bloom, is the increasing pressure for state planning of a comprehensive character. State planning as a potential answer to co-ordinational problems at the state and local levels is important but largely unexploited. The state planning agencies of the 1930's were for the most part transformed into postwar agencies to lure new industries to the states.

Another possible source of diminished tensions in federal–state relations is the prospect of a strengthened hand for the governor in the budgeting and administration of federal grants going to state agencies. The proposed intergovernmental co-operation act, which passed the United States Senate in 1966 but did not pass in the House, provided for greater flexibility in budgeting, greater information to the governor on federal administrative decisions and communications with state departments, and the possibility of consolidating some grants.

Another source of hope for the gradual reduction in the number and intensity of tension points in intergovernmental relations is found in the aging or maturing of federal aid programs with the passage of time. Considerable evidence exists in support of the hypothesis that the longer a federal aid program is in existence, the fewer the friction points in federal–state–local relations. One case in support of this hypothesis is found in the following quotation from the Illinois chapter in the Kestnbaum Commission's study of the impact of federal aid on states:

The atmosphere of administration in the federal grant programs has changed very greatly since 1936. The state officials are sure of themselves and they have confidence in their own staffs and in political support for their programs. The procedures have been mastered so that operations go forward with relative smoothness. Basic policies have been established and are not currently in question. There is not that dependence on federal representatives that there was when so many things were new. ... The federal representatives no longer work under such tight restrictions. Control systems are more relaxed, and there are few things other than basic plans and

budgets which require advance approval. Representatives of federal agencies know the state staffs and
have confidence in them. They are very much aware
that political forces within the state can be exerted
through Washington channels and they are chary of
intruding on political decisions. They respect the administrative integrity of the state administrative organizations and provide a consultant service on demand, rather than operate a higher headquarters.[31]

Administrators agonizing over the frictions and frayed
tempers of disagreements on definitions of "involvement
of the poor," "equal opportunity," or "workable program,"
ought to find some comfort in the prospects of time as a
great healer, even though it may be a kind of Job's comfort for those who must cope with the problems of the
present.

One other ray of hope, and perhaps the ultimate key to
the role of the state in the American governmental system,
is the consummation of the one-man-one-vote ideal in the
apportionment of state legislatures. If *Baker* v. *Carr* [32] and
Reynolds v. *Sims* [33] have the effect of turning the states
away from their rural ways and toward new and dynamic
urban ways, the day may come when the state's intervention in federal–local relations is not merely accepted
quietly by the cities but is actually welcomed. The metropolis needs help, and it is not too particular about
where it gets the help. Reapportionment and redistricting
state legislatures to make them strong spokesmen for
urban interests ought to result in many changes, but only
time will tell whether the urban path to Washington is
already too well traveled for any significant diversion of
that traffic to the state capitals.

V

State Governments and Metropolitan Areas

Daniel R. Grant

THE ASSERTION HAS BEEN MADE THAT THE future role of the states in the federal system depends in large measure on how they respond to the needs of metropolitan areas. Before considering specifically why this seems to be true, and what the prospects are for states to make such a response, it is important to make some preliminary distinctions in terminology. To do so runs the risk of appearing to dwell on the elementary or, perhaps, to engage in insignificant hair-splitting, but it is hoped that the reader's patient indulgence will be rewarded.

It is important to make a distinction between state–*city* relations and state–*metropolitan* relations since a city and a metropolitan area are not one and the same. The city is a legal creature of the state, granted a charter of incorporation specifying its powers and duties. The metropolitan area, on the other hand, is an economic–social–cultural community that is frequently two or three times the size of the core city and still growing. The metropolis contains core cities, suburban cities, unincorporated cities, frequently single-purpose and multi-purpose districts, one or more counties, and, on all too rare occasions, open space. The United States Bureau of the Census reported the existence of 212 of these "Standard Metropolitan Statistical Areas" in 1960 with an aggregate of more than 18,000 separate units of local government. Each metropolis has a certain internal unity, interdependence, and common set of needs, yet each is characterized by governmental fragmentation. These metropolitan areas constitute the heart of American life, with two-thirds of the population living there. But the metropolis is not a governmental entity; it is a happening still awaiting recognition by the state.

Thus state–city relations (and even state–urban relations) are not the same as state–metropolitan relations. State–city relations are important, but if state governors, legislators, and administrators see and deal with only these fragmented parts of whole metropolitan areas they will be ignoring what seems to be clearly the number one fact in the problems of modern living. Analogy is risky business, but it seems very much like performing major sugery on the arm or leg without checking before, during, and after the operation to determine the condition of the heart and lungs. It should be added parenthetically that it is common practice for not only the press but the literature of social science to use the terms "metropolis" and "city" as synonyms, making it an uphill battle for anyone who seeks to differentiate metropolitan problems in particular from city problems in general. Nevertheless, this is the distinction that will be made in the discussion that follows, focusing on three questions: (1) What are the uniquely *metropolitan* problems? (2) What *can* the states do about them? (3) What *will* the states do about them—probably?

What Are the Uniquely Metropolitan *Problems?*

The uniquely metropolitan problems differ from the more traditional urban or city problems in that they relate directly to the fragmented condition of the core city and its suburbs. In recent years, following repeated failures of reform efforts to consolidate or co-ordinate these fragmented patterns, some writers have been so bold as to suggest that these so-called metropolitan problems may exist only in the minds of the reformers, rather than constituting a matter of serious concern for the average metropolitan citizen. Yet this seems much like saying that tooth decay is not a problem if the voters consistently reject the fluoridation of water. There is always the danger, of course, of defining problems solely in terms of failure to coincide with some symmetrical ideal on an organization chart, but there is strong evidence that the difficulties associated with metropolitan fragmentation go far deeper than merely offending the political scientist's sense of symmetry.

A few years ago an analysis was made of 112 metropolitan surveys that were conducted separately over a period of three decades. Although the surveys had a wide variety of types of sponsorship, purpose, methodology, and final recommendations, they were in striking agreement in their descriptions of a common set of "problems" related to the governmental patchwork quilt in the metropolis.[1] This common set of uniquely metropolitan problems may be summarized as follows:

1. *Unequal Distribution of Financial Resources and Burdens.* Core cities complain bitterly of large suburban populations enjoying the benefits of expensive core city

services while living outside the reach of the city tax collector. Suburbs, on the other hand, complain of having to pay the ever-increasing costs of public education from a predominantly residential tax base. And almost every metropolitan area has some units of government, whether core city or suburb, whose tax resources are pitifully poor in comparison with other isolated well-off communities. Often the unit with the greatest tax resources will have the lowest tax rate.

2. *Unequal Service Levels.* For cities in the early stages of metropolitanism the suburbanite often suffers from the multiple menace of inadequate sewage disposal, fire protection, police protection, and water supply. In the older metropolitan areas some of the suburbs pride themselves on having a very high level of services while others find themselves in the underprivileged category.

3. *Absence of Area-wide Authority to Cope with Area-wide Problems.* Probably the most common complaint in the 112 metropolitan surveys concerned the serious consequences of the absence of any area-wide instrumentality to grapple with such problems as transit, water supply, sewers, public health, or planning. The fact that the surveys relied heavily on the old cliché about disease and crime being no respecter of political boundary lines might weaken their literary value, but it does not make the condition any less serious as a metropolitan problem. Fragmented approaches to the problems of metropolitan pollution—whether of the air or water—are classic examples of the uniquely metropolitan problem.

4. *Wasteful Duplication and Inefficiency.* The overlapping layers of local government, as well as those which do not overlap but do duplicate in a practical sense the facilities and personnel of many other nearby units of govern-

ment in the same area, were objects of strong criticism in the surveys. In many respects this problem has come to mean all things to all people involved in the politics of metropolitan reform, with erroneous visions of reduced taxes being held out to the readers of some of the reports. The more sophisticated surveyors, however, speak of this problem more realistically as one of waste of scarce personnel in top management positions and inability to exploit various potential economies of scale, including more specialized facilities, programs, and services that smaller units cannot afford. This, of course, is a different concept of "efficiency and economy" for the metropolitan community, and one that has little if anything to do with reduced taxes or with the stereotyped penny pinching in public expenditures.

5. *Inability of Citizens to Fix Responsibility for Local Government Action or Inaction.* In some respects the most serious problem of all is the dissipation and dispersion of citizen control of local government in the metropolitan community. The citizen bewildered at the maze of separate and overlapping units of governments, officials, agencies, and taxing authorities finds it impossible to pinpoint responsibility either for his major urban needs or for particular good service he may receive. If the essence of democracy is fixing responsibility for official deeds and misdeeds, with the accompanying popular rewards and punishments, then democracy is sadly deficient in most metropolitan areas.

6. *Political Segregation of Able Suburban Leaders from the Most Serious Urban (Core City) Problems.* While the problem of separating large numbers of business and civic leaders from the core city's governmental process is related to the preceding one, it deserves some special men-

tion. The fragmented structure of most metropolitan areas tends to give aid and comfort to the leader of the wealthy lily-white suburb who might be inclined to say to harassed core city politicians: "We in Azalea City are solving our problems of blight, poverty, and slum clearance; why can't you people in Gutter City do the same?" The other side of the same coin finds suburban leaders with a strong interest in a particular core city issue—or one in another suburb—but officially limited by his carpetbagger or nonresident status.

The foregoing problems have been stated more in terms of broad abstract types than in the tangible terms of congestion, blight, noise, and crime, that so often make up the agenda of urban problems. This is what is basically meant by *metropolitan* problems, which are a special category of problems making it exceedingly difficult even to come to grips with the agenda of urban problems.

What Can the States Do about Metropolitan Problems?

In considering what it is theoretically possible for the states to do about metropolitan problems it may be useful to engage in a little bit of pipe dreaming. If the states did whatever was necessary to meet metropolitan area needs—the problems just described—what would this involve? Presumably the Utopian answer would be for them to take affirmative action to bring the horse-and-buggy concepts of local government up to date with space-age realities. When applied to metropolitan areas "space age" takes on a dual meaning that includes the geographic space occupied by the *real* metropolitan community. Ideally the state would create a single, expandable, area-wide unit of metropolitan government to govern each metropolitan community. Smaller units of government would be retained only as necessary to protect important values of local diversity and to provide a sense of sub-community representation in the larger metropolitan government. The state would abolish all other units of local government within a metropolitan area. As unrealistic as this may seem in view of the temper of the times, it consists of little more than changing governmental structure to conform to the realities of community structure. It is true that in some cases the very large metropolitan areas are merging into "megalopoli," but this is hardly reason for the state to panic and leave the "1,400 governments" as they are. Nor are the problems of the very large megalopolis an adequate guide for state policy in designing local government structure for the majority of metropolitan areas which are much smaller and far less complicated.

If it is necessary to shift from the completely ideal to the ideal tempered with some degree of practicality, the state might make a two-pronged attack on the metropolitan problem: (1) For the smaller, newer, less complex metropolis the state might require—not merely authorize—strong programs of annexation, city–county consolidation, city–city consolidation, or other means of guaranteeing simple unified government for the metropolitan area. The record of school district consolidation in the past few decades is an outstanding example of what can be done by the effective use of state carrots and sticks. (2) For the larger, older, more complex metropolis the state might require—not merely authorize—either a strong federated or two-tier system of metropolitan government, or perhaps some kind of multi-purpose regional units of government. Either of the latter systems for the older and larger areas would have the effect of preserving most of the existing units of local government for "purely local" functions while creating a new area-wide layer of government for area-wide functions. The distinction between the state's *requiring* and merely *authorizing* such metropolitan systems of government is a deliberate one in recognition of the political realities of emotional opposition to their creation or, more specifically, to *any* change in the status quo.

Although this brief statement of what the states could do was prefaced with a reference to pipe dreaming, it is important to pause long enough to consider four specific cases, three in the United States and one in Canada, which take metropolitan reform out of the realm of total fantasy. In Baton Rouge, Miami, Nashville, and Toronto, variations of metropolitan government have been set up during the past two decades. The role of the state in each of these cases was far from ideal, particularly in the three United States cases, but at least the states held still for rather remarkable changes in the old order of things in the metropolis.

1. *Baton Rouge.* In 1947 a partial merger took place between the city of Baton Rouge and East Baton Rouge Parish, with populations of approximately 35,000 and 150,000, respectively. While it was not a complete consolidation, an interlocking-directorate device was used to make the city's governing body constitute the majority of the parish's governing body. A differential tax rate was provided for separate urban, industrial, and rural districts. The role of the state in this reorganization was limited to state legislative provision for the submission of a constitutional amendment to the people for a vote in 1946 on the creation of a City–Parish Charter Commis-

sion. The charter proposed by the commission in 1947 was
adopted by a simple majority of those voting in a
parish-wide referendum (7,012 to 6,705). It is worth noting that the Baton Rouge plan would undoubtedly have
been defeated if the state had required two separate majorities—inside and outside the city—as is so often the
case. A recent appraisal by Havard and Corty of the
Baton Rouge experience reports favorably on the values
of area-wide co-ordination growing out of the 1947 reorganization.[2]

2. *Miami.* After many years of struggling with their
mushrooming metropolitan growth, Miami and Dade
County created in 1957 a two-tier government preserving
the city of Miami and some twenty-six suburban munici-
palities, while transforming Dade County into an area-
wide metropolitan government. The action of the state of
Florida in this striking new development on the American
scene was similar to the role of Louisiana in the Baton
Rouge merger. In 1955 the Florida legislature agreed to
submit a proposed constitutional home rule amendment
for Dade County to a statewide referendum in 1956. In
the same year the legislature created a metropolitan charter board to draft a proposed charter for Dade County, for
subsequent vote in case the home rule amendment should
pass. Following statewide approval of the home rule
amendment, the proposed "metro charter" for Dade
County was approved by the narrow margin of 44,404 to
42,619, with only the simple majority in a countywide
referendum being required. It should be added, in any
evaluation of the role of the state, that the state judiciary
in Florida has played havoc with the taxing power of the
new Dade County metropolitan government, limiting it to
only the taxing powers of a county instead of assuming

the need and legitimacy of both municipal and county authority. Most observers of Dade County's early years of experience with metro are in agreement that this has been a serious limitation on the new government and a major contributing factor to its early political instability. Even so, Professor Edward Sofen and many other Miami observers conclude that it is worth the effort and that metro's future is bright.[3]

3. *Nashville.* In 1962 the voters of Nashville and Davidson County adoted a single metropolitan government to replace the existing city and county. The reform was in many respects traditional city–county consolidation, but the proposal was tailor-made to the unique needs of the Nashville metropolitan area. The new government provided for a tax differential with a higher rate in an expandable urban services district and a lower rate for the outer fringe not receiving urban services. The state of Tennessee has been involved in the Nashville consolidation in several ways and at several points in time during the decade preceding the consolidation. In 1953 an amendment was adopted to Tennessee's constitution (said previously to be the oldest unamended constitution in the world) authorizing the state legislature to provide for city–county consolidations. Following the local planning commission's proposal of a "Plan of Metropolitan Government for Nashville and Davidson County" the state legislature in 1957 adopted enabling legislation for this proposal and made it applicable to the four metropolitan counties in the state. When a 1958 effort in Nashville proved unsuccessful, the state legislature amended the enabling act in 1961 to make possible the new and successful Nashville effort in 1962. Perhaps more significant than the role of the state legislature in Tennessee has been

the role of the state judiciary. In sharp contrast to the rough judicial waters in Florida for Miami metro, the Nashville metropolitan experiment has received very sympathetic treatment on most major court tests. While it may be both cause and effect, this strong support from the state judiciary has contributed greatly to political stability for the new government in its early years. Early appraisals of the performance of Nashville metro have been highly favorable, although it is still too early for the development of much hard data on this subject.[4]

4. *Toronto.* A thirteen-city federation known as the Municipality of Metropolitan Toronto was created by enactment of the Ontario provincial parliament in 1953. Each of the cities retained certain powers over local matters and the metropolitan government was given responsibility on a regional basis for certain other functions, with a few activities being shared by both levels. It has often been said that the Toronto experience is not exportable to American metropolitan areas because it was simply imposed on the area by the provincial government without the requirement of a popular referendum. While this is true from the standpoint of what may be done at the local level, the Toronto experience may well be instructive to American states as they begin to feel their responsibility for the metropolitan problem. The Ontario Municipal Board is an administrative tribunal at the provincial level to hear applications and appeals concerning such municipal matters as annexation disputes. Following a petition in 1951 by the city of Toronto proposing amalgamation of the core city with its twelve suburbs, this provincial tribunal made an exhaustive study of the situation and, in addition to rejecting the request for amalgamation, it recommended to the provincial government a plan for feder-

ated government. Premier L. M. Frost reacted favorably to the plan and proposed legislation to that effect which was adopted by the provincial parliament in 1953. Several changes have been made since 1953 and all of them have been by action at the provincial level without the requirement of a local referendum. The latest change, effective January 1, 1967, is a thorough revision of the plan of federation, involving the merger of the thirteen cities into only six (the city of Toronto plus five suburban boroughs). Frank Smallwood and others who have studied the Toronto experience are in general agreement that there is virtually no sentiment for a return to the governmental structure in existence prior to 1953.[5]

Dr. Lorne Cumming, chairman of the Ontario Municipal Board at the time it made its 1953 report, has been a strong defender of the principle which holds that matters of metropolitan government structure should be decided at the provincial (state) level. In an unpublished speech to the Metropolitan Areas Study Commission for the Commonwealth of Virginia in 1967, Dr. Cumming contended that any metropolitan federation set up by voluntary local agreement, rather than by state action, would probably be weak or ineffective if indeed it could ever be brought into existence.

What Probably Will Be Done about the Metropolitan Problem?

If we judge only by past state action and inaction in the overwhelming majority of states, the answer to this question must be, "Virtually nothing." Roscoe C. Martin's book on the growing role of cities in the "expanded partnership" of federalism, cited in a preceding chapter by Professor Jewell, certainly gives no encouragement for a different answer.[6] In his chapter entitled "The Case of the Reluctant State," Martin delivers a stinging indictment of the states' failure "to react positively and effectively to the demands of a new age." He concludes:

> ... that state constitutions are outmoded and inflexible; that the legislatures, identified as the keystone of the democratic arch, are not representative; that resources, partly from deliberate choice, are inadequate; that the atmosphere is not congenial to the embrace of new programs; and that state horizons are severely limited by prevailing mythology. . . .
>
> [The] vast new problems of urban America are unique in the experience of the states, which react to them in an impatient and sometimes a truculent manner. Nothing would please the states more than for the cities and their problems to dematerialize into thin air. . . .
>
> Many observers believe that the states will prove equal to the challenges of the metropolitan age. The wish doubtless is father to the thought, and the thought perhaps to the hope; but one who allows hope to sire expectation ignores a considerable body of evidence.[7]

One might well ask whether the reapportionment revolution will prove Professor Martin's pessimistic appraisal of the states to be erroneous. Will these old political facts of life be changed at the state level by *Baker* v. *Carr* and *Reynolds* v. *Sims?* Some of the earliest journalistic comments on probable effects of state legislative reapportionment on a one-man/one-vote basis indicated that metropolitan reform would be a logical result of more urban oriented legislatures. It is still too early to know, of course, but it is already evident that it is the suburbs and not the core cities that will gain the most from state legislative reapportionment. While core cities were generally under-represented from a moderate amount to a great deal, the suburban areas had come to be far more acutely underrepresented. It was the rapid growth after World War II which made the difference. One close follower of state reapportionment activity has described this situation as follows: "The United States is an urban nation, but not a big-city nation. The suburbs own the future." [8]

Thus, the result of reapportionment will not be a simple shift from rural to urban control of the state legislatures. A more accurate picture is probably a complex power pattern of shifting alliances depending upon the particular issue of the moment. We can quite probably expect rural small town alliances with metropolitan suburbs on such subjects as core city taxes, welfare legislation, annexation, and metro-type governments, with a negative stance on these subjects. On the other hand, core city and suburbs should be expected to stick together on such matters as increasing state aid for education, expressways, and mass transit, and perhaps for home rule legislation. In any case there is certainly no guarantee or even strong prospect that replacing rural representatives with suburban representatives will result in state action for significant structural change in the fragmented government of metropolitan areas.

In describing what he called "the withering away of the city," [9] York Willbern referred to the traditional central city as definitely on the way out. He considered the question of whether or not a new unit of government would be created to provide local self-government for the new and much enlarged metropolitan agglomeration. His answer is

"No," and the political phenomenon which he describes as not far down the road is a veritable jungle of complex vertical and horizontal administrative, political, and legal relationships. I would suggest that the title of Willbern's metropolis of tomorrow be "The Intergovernmental Megalopolity," with the national government providing strong functional leadership but with state officials also involved.

Willbern predicts that the career bureaucrat, the expert staff man, will have growing professional influence in this kind of governmental system. Only highly specialized personnel will be able to carry on the negotiations necessary to comply with the elaborate system of policy and regulations involved. The need for professional generalists among all the specialists will be increasingly urgent. The urban planner's role will undoubtedly be increased, with his training orienting him toward the general interest and the broader viewpoint. But there will be no real metropolitan political entity as such, according to Willbern. My own appraisal of the prospects of the metropolitan community is not quite so pessimistic. I am neither so gloomy about the role of the state as Professor Martin, nor so pessimistic about the future structure of the metropolitan community as Professor Willbern. But neither, I hope, am I naïvely optimistic. I personally believe the outcome is still open—"up for grabs," so to speak. It is neither too late for the states to turn away from their basically anti-metropolitan stance, nor is it too late for the creation of rational metropolitan government in the great majority of cases.

Some of the evidence for this position is rather impressionistic and we must admit that a considerable amount of evidence goes against it. Nevertheless, there is far too much ferment, civic leader interest, investigation of metro schemes, and general dissatisfaction with where the metropolitan area is and where it is headed, to be written off as mere exercises in futility. The almost daily pilgrimages of visiting delegations from other metropolitan areas to observe the operation of Nashville's new metro government does not sound as if consolidation is a dead issue. The voters' adoption in July, 1967, of a unified government for Jacksonville (Florida) and Duval County, similar in many respects to the Nashville plan, is a case in point.

The bulk of the experience of metropolitan reformers during the past forty years would seem to support those who predict the development of many headless and formless "intergovernmental megalopolities," rather than rational area-wide local governments for metropolitan communities. Yet it is just possible that some state legislatures, especially in the southern and western regions where local government has not yet become so complex, may decide to design and make mandatory a new and workable unit of local self-government for the metropolitan community. The chances for such legislative action are better for the smaller and newly emerging metropolitan areas than for the larger and older ones. Similarly, the chances are better if a governor should provide vigorous leadership in this direction. And certainly there can be no question about the adequacy of the state's legal authority, given the political will, to take such action.

We end, therefore, where we began. The metropolitan area is not now a creature of the state. The metropolitan area in most cases can become a creature of the state, or of the national government (with the states being by-passed), or of both (through federal–state "partner-

ship"), or of neither (by continued inability or unwillingness to provide a formal structure for area-wide
self-government for the metropolitan community). The
conclusion is no less probable because it may sound to
some like the prophecy of a high school valedictory: the
action of state governments in the next ten to twenty years
will determine the future of metropolitan government,
which, in turn, may well determine the future of state
government.

Notes

Chapter I

1. U.S. Congress, Senate Subcommittee on Executive Reorganization, Committee on Government Operations, *Federal Role in Urban Affairs,* 89th Cong., 2d sess., Part 3, pp. 550 ff., 671 ff., 764.

2. "'I knew it,' said Eustace. 'Everyone who wants to do good to the human race always ends in universal bullying.'" Aldous Huxley, *Time Must Have a Stop* (1944, Berkeley ed., 1963), p. 71.

3. Morton Grodzins, "Centralization and Decentralization in the American Federal System," in *A Nation of States: Essays on the American Federal System* (Chicago: Rand McNally & Co., 1961, 1963), pp. 18, 19. The view of American federalism presented by Grodzins and Daniel Elazar has been sharply attacked by Harry N. Scheiber, in *The Condition of American Federalism: An Historian's View,* U.S. Congress, Senate, Subcommittee on Intergovernmental Relations, Committee on Government Operations, 89th Cong., 2d sess., Oct. 15, 1966, committee print.

4. Herbert S. Klein, in his *Slavery in the Americas: A Comparative Study of Virginia and Cuba* (Chicago: The University of Chicago Press, 1967), has shown how Virginia developed

its customary law to degrade the slave to the condition of a chattel.

5. James M. Quigley, "Federal Water Pollution Control Program," in *Proceedings of the State and Interstate Water Pollution Control Administrators in Joint Meeting with the Conference of State Sanitary Engineers* (Washington, Department of Health, Education, and Welfare, 1962), p. 9. Of course, a bureaucrat's threat is not the final word; obstruction may be exercised through Congress as well as through the states, and state political forces are active in both.

6. Daniel J. Elazar, *American Federalism: A View from the States* (New York: Thomas Y. Crowell, 1966), p. 60.

7. In his article "The Case for a Stronger National Government" (in *A Nation of States,* note 3 above), Harry V. Jaffa argues that the domestic concerns of governments within the United States vitally affect the national security and ends up by quoting Hamilton favorably on the "illimitable nature" of the powers of the central government. Hamilton said: "The power of making that provision [for national defense and public peace against foreign *and domestic* violence] ought to know no other bounds than the exigencies of the nation and the resources of the community" (p. 116). Once this argument is accepted, the need for any differentiation between governmental powers is at an end.

8. Jack E. Holmes, Walter N. Lambert, and Nelson M. Robinson, *The Structure of County Government in Tennessee* (Knoxville: Bureau of Public Administration, University of Tennessee, 1966), *passim.*

9. Alexander Heard, ed., *State Legislatures in American Politics* (Englewood Cliffs, N.J.: Prentice–Hall, 1966), p. 156.

10. The disadvantages of our highly localized system are discussed in Lewis Mayers, *The American Legal System; The Administration of Justice in the United States by Judicial, Administrative, Military and Arbitral Tribunals,* rev. ed. (New York: Harper & Row, 1964), pp. 42 ff.

Chapter II

1. Paul T. David and Ralph Eisenberg, *Devaluation of the Urban and Suburban Vote* (Charlottesville: Bureau of Public Administration, University of Virginia, 1961), pp. 9, 15.

2. Donald S. Strong, *Urban Republicanism in the South* (University, Ala.: Bureau of Public Administration, University of Alabama, 1960), *passim.*

3. Paul T. David and Ralph Eisenberg, *State Legislative Redistricting: Major Issues in the Wake of Judicial Decision* (Chicago: Public Administration Service, 1962), p. 20.

4. Malcolm E. Jewell, "The Place Method in State Legislative Elections" (Paper delivered at the National Conference on Government, Boston, Mass., Nov. 13–16, 1966).

5. *Tennessee Code Annotated,* 3–101.

6. The Florida and Georgia controversies are discussed in George J. Mauer, ed., *Evolving Issues and Patterns of State Legislative Redistricting in Large Metropolitan Areas* (Oklahoma City: Institute of Metropolitan Studies, Oklahoma City University, 1966).

7. Thomas R. Dye, "Malapportionment and Public Policy in the States," *Journal of Politics,* vol. 27 (August, 1965), p. 588. See also Richard I. Hofferbert, "The Relation Between Public Policy and Some Structural and Environmental Variables in American States," *American Political Science Review,* vol. 60 (March, 1966), pp. 73–82, and David Brady and Douglas Edmonds, "The Effects of Malapportionment on Policy Output in the American States," mimeographed (Laboratory for Political Research, University of Iowa, 1966).

8. Glendon Schubert and Charles Press, "Measuring Apportionment," *American Political Science Review,* vol. 58 (June and December, 1964), pp. 302–37, 966–70.

9. David and Eisenberg, *Devaluation,* pp. 7–10.

10. Dye, "Malapportionment," p. 599.

11. H. D. Price, "Florida: Politics and 'Pork Choppers,'"

in Malcolm E. Jewell, ed., *The Politics of Reapportionment* (New York: Atherton Press, 1962), p. 89.

12. Roscoe C. Martin, *The Cities and the Federal System* (New York: Atherton Press, 1965), pp. 72–74.

13. Martin, *Cities and Federal System*, p. 75.

14. Martin, *Cities and Federal System*, p. 80–81.

Chapter III

1. *State Legislatures in American Politics: Report of the Twenty-ninth American Assembly* (Harriman, N.Y.: Arden House, 1966), p. 5.

2. *State Legislatures in Politics*, p. 7.

3. *Book of the States, 1948–49* (Chicago: Council of State Governments), p. 108; *ibid., 1966–67*, pp. 43, 48–49.

4. Malcolm E. Jewell, *Legislative Representation in the Contemporary South* (Durham, N.C.: Duke University Press, 1967), p. 32.

5. James David Barber, *The Lawmakers* (New Haven, Conn.: Yale University Press, 1965), pp. 27, 121.

6. Barber, *Lawmakers*, pp. 67–115.

7. Jewell, "Legislative Representation," pp. 28–39.

8. *State Legislatures in Politics*, p. 6.

9. *Book of the States, 1948–49*, pp. 115–17; *ibid., 1962–63*, p. 66; *ibid., 1966–67*, p. 79.

10. *State Legislatures in Politics*, pp. 7–8.

11. *Book of the States, 1966–67*, p. 69.

12. *State Legislatures in Politics*, p. 8.

13. *Book of the States, 1966–67*, pp. 72–78.

14. Arlene T. Shadoan, *Organization, Role, and Staffing of State Budget Offices* (Lexington: Bureau of Business Research, University of Kentucky, 1961), pp. 79–84.

15. Shadoan, *Organization*, pp. 77–78.

16. Shadoan, *Organization*, p. 94.

17. Clifton McCleskey, *The Government and Politics of Texas*, 2d ed. (Boston: Little, Brown & Co., 1966), pp. 228–29.

18. *State Legislatures in Politics*, p. 4.

Chapter IV

1. 252 U.S. 416 (1920).

2. 379 U.S. 241 (1964).

3. As quoted in Sidney Wise, ed., *Issues, 1965–66: Documents in Current American Government and Politics* (New York: Thomas Y. Crowell, 1965), p. 11.

4. Wise, *Issues*, p. 11.

5. Wise, *Issues*, p. 11.

6. John W. Burgess, "The American Commonwealth: Changes in Its Relation to the Nation," *Political Science Quarterly*, vol. 1 (March, 1886), p. 34.

7. Charles E. Merriam, "Metropolitan Regions" (Paper delivered at the University of Chicago, March 20, 1928, in *University Record*, April, 1928), as quoted in W. Brooke Graves, *American State Government*, Third Edition (Boston: D. C. Heath & Co., 1946), p. 943.

8. Luther Gulick, "Reorganization of the State" *Civil Engineering*, vol. 4 (August, 1933), pp. 420–22.

9. George C. S. Benson, *The New Centralization* (New York: Farrar & Rinehart, Inc., 1941), p. 157.

10. Leonard D. White, *The States and the Nation* (Baton Rouge: Louisiana State University Press, 1953), p. 3.

11. James Jackson Kilpatrick, *The Sovereign States*, as quoted in Robert B. Dishman, *The State of the Union* (New York: Charles Scribner's Sons, 1965), p. 50.

12. *Congressional Digest*, vol. 40 (August–September, 1961), p. 211.

13. *Congressional Digest*, vol. 41 (May, 1962), p. 141.

14. As quoted in *Report of the U.S. Commission on Intergovernmental Relations* (Washington, Government Printing Office, 1955), p. 123.

15. *Christian Science Monitor*, Jan. 6, 1966.

16. Government Expenditures Committee, National Association of Manufacturers, *The Federal Budget for 1967* (New York, 1966), pp. 3–4.

17. U.S. Commission on Intergovernmental Relations, *A Report to the President for Transmittal to the Congress* (Washington, 1955), p. 118.

18. U.S. Commission on Intergovernmental Relations, *The Impact of Federal Grants–in–Aid on the Political Structure and Functions of State and Local Government* (Washington, 1955), p. 19.

19. Harry W. Reynolds, "Merit Controls, the Hatch Act, and Personnel Standards of Intergovernmental Relations," *Annals of the American Academy of Political and Social Science,* vol. 359 (May, 1965), pp. 81–93.

20. Reynolds, "Merit Controls," p. 86.

21. *Impact of Federal Grants–in–Aid,* p. 8.

22. *Impact of Federal Grants–in–Aid,* p. 7.

23. *State Government Organization and Federal Grant–in–Aid Program Requirements,* A Report to the Governors' Conference, Hershey, Pa., July 1–4, 1962 (Chicago, Council of State Governments), p. 2.

24. *State Government Organization,* p. 28.

25. *A Report to the President,* p. 129.

26. *Impact of Federal Grants–in–Aid,* pp. 18–19.

27. *A Report to the President,* p. 67.

28. On this point see Charles E. Gilbert and David G. Smith, "Emerging Patterns of Federalism in Health, Education, and Welfare" (Paper delivered at the sixty-second annual meeting of the American Political Science Association, New York, September 10, 1966), p. 4.

29. Norman Beckman, "A New Perspective of Federal–State Relations" (Paper delivered at the Conference on State Planning, Cornell University, March 23–24, 1966), p. 1.

30. Beckman, "A New Perspective," p. 28.

31. *Impact of Federal Grants–in–Aid,* pp. 9–10.

32. 369 U.S. 186 (1962).

33. 377 U.S. 533 (1964).

Chapter V

1. See Daniel R. Grant, "General Metropolitan Surveys: A Summary," in *Metropolitan Surveys: A Digest* (New York, Government Affairs Foundation, 1958), pp. 1–24.

2. William C. Havard, Jr., and Floyd L. Corty, *Rural–Urban Consolidation: The Merger of Governments in the Baton Rouge Area* (Baton Rouge: Louisiana State University Press, 1964).

3. Edward Sofen, *The Miami Metropolitan Experiment* (Bloomington, Indiana University Press, 1963).

4. See Roscoe C. Martin, *Metropolis in Transition: Local Government Adaptation to Changing Urban Needs* (Washington: U.S. Housing and Home Finance Agency, 1963), chap. IX, and Daniel R. Grant, "A Comparison of Predictions and Experience with Nashville 'Metro,'" *Urban Affairs Quarterly*, vol. 1 (September, 1965), pp. 35–54. For two studies of the politics of adoption, see Brett W. Hawkins, *Nashville Metro: The Politics of City–County Consolidation* (Nashville: Vanderbilt University Press, 1966), and David A. Booth, *Metropolitics: The Nashville Consolidation* (East Lansing: Institute for Community Development and Services, Michigan State University, 1963).

5. Frank Smallwood, *Metro Toronto: A Decade Later* (Toronto: Bureau of Municipal Research, 1963). See also Harold Kaplan, "Politics and Policy-making in Metropolitan Toronto," *Canadian Journal of Economics and Political Science*, vol. 31 (November, 1965), pp. 538–51, and Daniel R. Grant, "Metro's Three Faces," *National Civic Review*, vol. 55 (June, 1966), pp. 317–24.

6. Roscoe C. Martin, *The Cities and the Federal System* (New York: Atherton Press, 1965).

7. Martin, *Cities and Federal System*, pp. 79, 80, 81.

8. William J. D. Boyd, "Suburbia Takes Over," *National Civic Review*, vol. 54 (June, 1965), pp. 294–98.

9. York Willbern, *The Withering Away of the City* (University, Ala.: University of Alabama Press, 1964).

Index